ELVIS PRESLEY

IN THE MOVIES

ELVIS PRESLEY

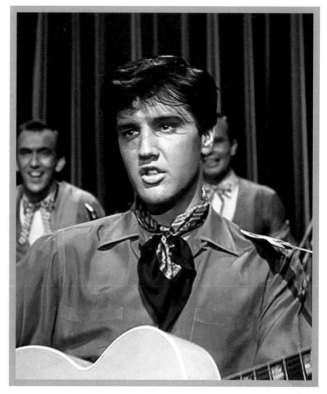

IN THE MOVIES

A RETROSPECTIVE BY TIMOTHY KNIGHT

METRO BOOKS
NEW YORK

DESIGNER: Les Krantz with Julie Nor
CONTRIBUTING WRITERS:
Ken DuBois, Michael Fox, Pam Grady, Dennis Kwiatkowski, Sheila Lane,
Debra Ott, James Plath, Tim Sika and Christopher Varaste
COPY EDITORS: Katherine Hinkebein, Janet W. Morris
PHOTO EDITOR: Thomas Jensen
DVD DOCUMENTARY:
Les Krantz (Executive Producer), Jack Piantino (Video Editor)
Kristie Back (Musical Selections)

METRO BOOKS
122 Fifth Avenue
New York, NY 10011

ISBN-13: 978-1-4351-1855-3

Library of Congress data available on request

Printed and bound in China by PWGS

1 3 5 7 9 10 8 6 4 2

DEDICATION

For my brother Kevin

ACKNOWLEDGMENTS

I received invaluable advice and assistance from many people while working on this book/documentary package. First and foremost, I am especially grateful to Les Krantz, my mentor and frequent collaborator, whose persistence and vision made *Elvis Presley in the Movies* possible. Thanks also to copy editors Katherine Hinkebein and Janet W. Morris, designer Julie Nor and photo editor Thomas Jensen for their exemplary work. Kudos to Jack Piantino and Kristie Back for skillfully assembling and editing the accompanying documentary; to Jeff Joseph of Sabucat Productions for providing the feature film footage; and to Susan Hormuth for providing the newsreel footage. Finally, my sincere thanks to everyone at Barnes & Noble for their good judgment and staunch support; I am especially indebted to Cynthia Barrett, Mark Levine and Peter Norton.

It was my great good fortune to work with a crackerjack team of writers on *Elvis Presley in the Movies*. I cannot thank them enough for their sterling contributions and prodigious work ethic. I tip my hat in gratitude to Ken Dubois, Michael Fox, Pam Grady, Dennis Kwiatkowski, Sheila Lane, Debra Ott, James Plath, Tim Sika and Christopher Varaste.

Scores of online and print sources were checked and cross-checked in the researching and writing of *Elvis Presley in the Movies*. Aside from the websites www.elvispresley.com.au, imdb.com, tcm.com and rottentomatoes.com, the *New York Times* online archive and the Academy Awards database, the following books provided the bulk of the information on Presley's life and career: *The Colonel: The Extraordinary Story of Colonel Tom Parker and Elvis Presley* by Alanna Nash (Simon & Schuster, 2003); *Elvis: A Celebration: Images of Elvis Presley From The Elvis Presley Archives At Graceland* by Mike Evans (Ballantine, 2002); *Elvis and Me* by Priscilla Beaulieu Presley with Sandra Harmon (Putnam, 1985); *Elvis! Elvis! Elvis! The King and His Movies* by Peter Guttmacher (MetroBooks, 1997); *Elvis: From Memphis to Hollywood: Memories from My Twelve Years with Elvis Presley* by Alan Fortas (Popular Culture, Inc., 1992); *Elvis: Still Taking Care of Business* by Sonny West with Marshall Terrill (Triumph Books, 2007); *Elvis Presley: A Life In Music: The Complete Recording Sessions* by Ernst Jorgensen (St. Martin's Press, 1998); The *Inner Elvis: A Psychological Biography of Elvis Aaron Presley by* Peter Whitmer (Hyperion, 1996); and two books by Peter Guralnick: *Careless Love: The Unmaking of Elvis Presley (*Little, Brown and Company, 1999) and *Last Train to Memphis: The Rise of Elvis Presley (*Little, Brown and Company, 1994).

TABLE OF CONTENTS

INTRODUCTION

Although he starred in 31 films and was ranked a top-10 box office draw for six consecutive years, Elvis Presley has never gotten his full due from film critics and historians, who often dismiss him as a singer, moonlighting on the silver screen, rather than a bona fide movie star. Yet the Tupelo, Mississippi, native known as "The King" enjoyed far greater success on-screen than any rock and roll star who followed his lead to Hollywood. And while he may have never achieved the artistic heights of his idols, Marlon Brando and James Dean, Presley nevertheless took on challenging, multifaceted roles that revealed him to be capable of far more than swaggering his way across the screen. In such films as *King Creole* (1958) and *Wild in the Country* (1961), Presley demonstrates an impressive emotional facility opposite top-notch actors like Walter Matthau and Tuesday Weld, respectively.

Perhaps if he had ignored the Svengali-esque counsel of his manager, Colonel Tom Parker, and continued starring in dramatic, commercially risky films, instead of formulaic musical comedies,

PRESLEY'S GREATEST PERFORMANCES

VINCE EVERETT
Jailhouse Rock (1957)

Presley is magnetism personified as the rebellious antihero of *Jailhouse Rock* (1957), which cemented his screen stardom and smashed box office records across the country and abroad. Then just 22 years old, the rock and roll legend smolders with white-hot intensity opposite his co-star, the ill-fated Judy Tyler, who died in a car accident soon after filming completed. In 2004, the National Film Registry selected *Jailhouse Rock* for preservation as "a culturally, historically or aesthetically significant film."

DANNY FISHER
King Creole (1958)

Taking on a role once intended for James Dean, Presley silenced his doubters by giving what is arguably his most fully realized performance as a New Orleans singer, ensnared with the mob, in *King Creole* (1958). The acting novice impressed Academy Award–winning director Michael Curtiz, who helped Presley develop the dramatic chops to portray the mercurial yet vulnerable Danny Fisher.

PACER BURTON
Flaming Star (1960)

Playing the son of a Kiowa mother and a white father, Presley gives a sensitive performance in Don Siegel's flawed but compelling western, *Flaming Star* (1960). One of Presley's few box office flops, *Flaming Star* received mixed notices when it opened in December 1960. Today, it's regarded as one of his better films. As for Presley's performance, film critic/historian David Thomson rightly praises it as "genuine."

Presley might have become as electrifying an actor as he was a performer. But for most of his 13-year film career, Presley starred in lighthearted escapist fare that left many critics cold. That said, the best of these musical comedies — *Blue Hawaii* (1961), *Girls! Girls! Girls!* (1962) and *Viva Las Vegas* (1964) — are infectiously entertaining popcorn films, brimming with catchy songs and exuberant energy. Only the most hardened curmudgeon can resist Presley's sizzling duet with Ann-Margret in *Viva Las Vegas*. Or his easygoing rapport with Shelley Fabares in *Clambake* (1967), one of three films he made with the actress he called his favorite leading lady. Granted, many of Presley's films are eminently forgettable, but he's effortlessly charismatic and likable, even when the material is mediocre. Like all the great stars, he holds the screen by sheer force of personality.

Elvis Presley in the Movies pays homage to the pop culture icon who burned up the screen without ever breaking a sweat. Enjoy!

GLENN TYLER
Wild in the Country (1961)

Presley effectively portrays a troubled young man who gets romantically involved with his therapist (Hope Lange) in *Wild in the Country* (1961), Clifford Odets' adaptation of J.R. Salamanca's novel *The Lost Country*. Despite its impressive pedigree in front of and behind the camera, *Wild in the Country* is an uneven film that's chiefly notable for Presley's understated performance in a difficult role.

WALTER GULICK
Kid Galahad (1962)

The King dons boxing gloves and steps into the ring as prizefighter in *Kid Galahad* (1962), a musicalized remake of the 1937 Warner Bros. film. To portray the title character convincingly, Presley trained with former world welterweight champion Mushy Callahan. He's impressive in the ring, but Presley shines brightest when he's singing *Kid Galahad*'s six songs, especially "King of the Whole Wide World," which he performs during the film's title sequence.

LUCKY JACKSON
Viva Las Vegas (1964)

Except for *Jailhouse Rock* (1957), no other film captures the essence of Presley's mega-watt charisma as well as *Viva Las Vegas* (1964). Paired with the equally magnetic Ann-Margret, Presley gives one of his most energetic performances as Lucky Jackson, a racecar driver determined to win both the Las Vegas Grand Prix *and* the heart of Rusty (Ann-Margret). Offscreen, sparks flew between Presley and his sexy leading lady; the stars' year long relationship ultimately turned into a lifelong friendship.

PART 1

1956-1958

ELVIS PRESLEY: 1956-1958

Elvis Presley seemed to have been born at the right place at the right time. In the 1950s, the early seeds of sexual and social revolution were being sown. Dr. Alfred Kinsey had shocked the world with his reports on male and female sexuality in 1948 and 1953, respectively. In 1953, Marilyn Monroe had appeared in the first issue of Hugh Hefner's *Playboy* magazine. In 1954, the landmark Supreme Court decision in *Brown v. Board of Education* had called for an end to racial segregation in public schools. By 1956, the United States, or at least its teenagers, seemed more than ready to find an outlet for these mounting tensions. Much to their parents' consternation, those teenagers found it in the racy live and television appearances of a sharecropper's son named Elvis Presley.

PRESLEY'S LEADING LADIES, 1956-1958

DOLORES HART
Loving You (1957)

Big things were predicted for Hart, the talented and beautiful ingénue who co-starred in Presley's second and third films, *Loving You* (1957) and *King Creole* (1958). But the actress once compared to Grace Kelly shocked Hollywood by abandoning her film career to become a Roman Catholic nun in 1963. All told, Hart starred in 10 films, including *Where the Boys Are* (1960) and earned a Tony Award nomination for her performance in the 1959 Broadway hit, *The Pleasure of His Company*. Years later, when asked why she left Hollywood for the cloistered life of the convent, the Reverend Mother Dolores Hart replied, "I have a contract with God."

CAROLYN JONES
King Creole (1958)

Baby boomers of a certain age remember Jones as Morticia, the matriarch of the classic sitcom *The Addams Family*, which aired on ABC from 1964 to 1966. Prior to donning the black fright wig and form-fitting costume she wore in every episode of that series, Jones had made a name for herself on the big screen. She had been nominated for a Best Supporting Actress Academy Award for *The Bachelor Party* (1957) and starred opposite Frank Sinatra in *A Hole in the Head* (1959). After *The Addams Family*, she continued working in television and film until her death in 1983.

LIZABETH SCOTT
Loving You (1957)

British film historian Leslie Halliwell memorably described the husky-voiced Scott as "a box office concoction of blonde hair, defiant expression and immobile upper lip." During her brief Hollywood career — she made just 21 films in 12 years — Scott made a name for herself as one of film noir's most alluring femme fatales. Except for a cameo appearance in *Pulp* (1972), the star of *The Strange Love of Martha Ivers* (1946) and *Dead Reckoning* (1947) never made another film after *Loving You*.

Perhaps this was largely because Presley rebelled against the era's conformist status quo with swaggering gusto. He wore long hair and sideburns. He dressed in flashy pink and yellow suits. As a musician, he combined country and hillbilly music with gospel and blues to create what would become known as "rockabilly." His hips seemed to naturally gyrate and swivel when he sang in public — even, rather scandalously, when he was singing gospel. This trademark musical style — a kind of radical racial integration all its own, fueled by his innate sensuality — would catapult him to stardom in 1956, earning him his first gold record and a movie deal with Paramount Pictures.

Only a few months earlier, Presley had signed with Colonel Tom Parker, a legendary manager for artists Eddy Arnold and Frank Snow and described by various friends as "something between W.C. Fields and P.T. Barnum." Parker had been instrumental in negotiating Presley's deal with RCA Records — which paid Presley an unprecedented $5,000 bonus — and in establishing the publishing firm that would become Elvis Presley Music, Inc. In early 1956, "Heartbreak Hotel" hit the airwaves and eventually shot to number one on the *Billboard* pop and country charts.

Amid appearances on *The Milton Berle Show*, *The Steve Allen Show*, *The Ed Sullivan Show*, and live performances that saw hysterical teenage girls screaming and crashing through barricades, Presley signed a three-picture deal with Hal Wallis and Paramount Pictures, who then loaned him out to Twentieth Century Fox for his first picture, *Love Me Tender* (1956).

By late 1956, a kind of "Presley-mania" was taking hold across the United States. September 26 was declared "Elvis Presley Day" in his hometown of Tupelo, Mississippi. His name and likeness were licensed for all manner of merchandise, from T-shirts to stuffed hound dogs. The marketing frenzy seemed to presage the boy-band hysteria of the late '80s and '90s, and grossed $22 million in sales.

By 1957, the boy who had been born on the "wrong side of the tracks" could now afford to buy himself and his family a bit of luxury and security: Graceland Mansion. Graceland was purchased for all of $102,500 in March of that year, but Presley, on tour around the United States and Canada, would not get to sleep in his own home until June.

In December, the Presley family would spend their first — and last — Christmas together in Graceland. That month, Presley received his military draft notice, and in January, he reported for duty in the U.S. Army. In March, he was stationed at Ford Hood for basic training. His parents, Vernon and Gladys, with whom he'd been almost preternaturally close since childhood, soon followed. Because army regulations allowed them to be classified as his dependents, Presley was permitted to live off post in temporary housing with them. Fears that his military service would impede or cut short his career were assuaged with the release of his fourth film, *King Creole* (1958), and fan letters that continued to pour in by the thousands.

By August 1958, however, Presley's mother, Gladys, had fallen ill and she returned to Memphis, where she was hospitalized with acute hepatitis. Presley was granted emergency leave from the army and stayed with her for two days. When he returned to Graceland to rest, however, leaving Vernon to remain at her bedside, Gladys passed away at age 46. At her funeral, the Blackwood Brothers sang "Rock of Ages" and "Precious Memories." As both the assembled press and fans watched, Presley sobbed, "Oh, God, everything I have is gone." Though military service and his music career forced him to press on, it is likely that Presley never fully recovered from the loss.

"I'd probably starve to death. If it ever did happen, and I don't think it would, I'd make a serious try to keep on top in the movies."

— Presley, when asked what he'd do if rock and roll ever died

Lizabeth Scott and Presley in *Loving You* (1957).

Top: Presley in *Loving You* (1957). Bottom: Debra Paget, Presley's first leading lady, in *Love Me Tender* (1956).

LOVE ME TENDER (1956)

TWENTIETH CENTURY FOX

DIRECTOR: ROBERT D. WEBB

SCREENPLAY: ROBERT BUCKNER

PRINCIPAL CAST: ELVIS PRESLEY (CLINT RENO), RICHARD EGAN (VANCE RENO), DEBRA PAGET (CATHY RENO), WILLIAM CAMPBELL (BRETT RENO), NEVILLE BRAND (MIKE GAVIN) AND MILDRED DUNNOCK (MARTHA RENO)

Movie trailers for *Love Me Tender* created the impression that the young rock and roll sensation would appear in every frame of the film, but Elvis Presley's first acting role is a supporting one. He plays Clint Reno, a farm kid whose older brother is the real focus of the film, a western drama with few opportunities for any character to swivel his hips or strum a guitar. The songs that *Love Me Tender* does feature are performed by Presley with his signature bravado in the film's lighthearted moments. *Love Me Tender* also requires the rock and roll idol to *act*, rather than coast on personality, even though Presley didn't have any time to hone his dramatic skills. He therefore had no choice but to approach the task naturally, and that turns out to be the most winning element in *Love Me Tender*.

Set in 1865, *Love Me Tender* centers on Vance Reno (Richard Egan), the leader of a small band of Confederate soldiers who learn the war is over just after they've robbed

Top: Clint Reno (Presley) is overjoyed to see his older brother, long feared dead. Bottom: Vance Reno (Richard Egan) returns home to see Cathy (Debra Paget), whose picture he has carried with him throughout the Civil War.

a Union train and escaped to divvy up the spoils of war. With his share of the money, Vance heads home to reunite with his family and his betrothed, who are both thrilled and stunned to see him, as they believed he had been killed in battle. In Vance's absence, his younger brother Clint (Presley) has married Vance's fiancée Cathy (Debra Paget); faced with both Reno brothers, she becomes deeply conflicted about her feelings. Vance quickly makes plans: For Clint and Cathy's sake, he'll leave most of his money with the family and head out west, never to return. Before he can leave, the authorities confront him about the stolen payroll, and he must convince his entire gang to return their shares or face imprisonment. But the bigger problems for Vance are Cathy, whom he still loves deeply, and his kid brother Clint, whose jealousy and suspicion threaten to shatter their family bond.

True to the best of the western genre, the action in *Love Me Tender* takes place mostly on horseback, with guns blazing, loyalties shifting, and a secret hideout that becomes the setting for the film's dramatic climax. Musical scenes occur early in the film — there's no time for a song once the chase is on — and blend nicely into the story, with Presley performing a couple of front-porch serenades for the Reno family and swinging through two more from the stage of a country festival. Anachronisms are few; aside from Presley's trademark pompadour and a bit of swivel, *Love Me Tender* is built on

Top: With his reunited family around him, Clint Reno delivers a front porch performance. Middle: Clint Reno serenades his mother, Martha (Mildred Dunnock), with "Love Me Tender." Bottom: Reunited, Clint explains to Vance how he feels about Cathy.

Clint sees Cathy and Martha off to the local festival.

the realism one expects from a big-budget western, with attention given to period details and gorgeous rural locations. Even the title song, rewritten with new words, is fairly authentic: a Civil War ballad known previously as "Aura Lee."

The most experienced actor in *Love Me Tender* is Richard Egan, who had appeared in 34 films before taking the role of Vance Reno. He recognized that Presley's lack of experience was an asset and encouraged him to just be himself. Debra Paget, who warmed to Presley on the set but declined to date him, also helped Presley by delivering an emotional performance to which Presley could respond. Paget had appeared in films regularly since the age of 14, and Presley was one of her many fans; in fact, she was the "It" girl of the moment, appearing on-screen in another hit film, Cecil B. DeMille's *The Ten Commandments* (1956), at the same time *Love Me Tender* was released. Absent from the cast is Presley's real-life band, who would appear in many of his films in the years to come. Although the band made the trip from Memphis to Los Angeles to audition, the producers rejected them, saying they just weren't "hillbilly" enough.

Shooting for *Love Me Tender* began in September 1956, just three months before the film was scheduled for release. Nervous about the project and unsure of the

"I know you and Cathy used to be kind of fond of each other but, well, you ain't got no hard feelings against either one of us now, have ya?"

— Clint Reno (Elvis Presley) to Vance Reno (Richard Egan)

filmmaking process, Presley had memorized the entire script, instead of just the scenes in which he appears. The seriousness with which he approached the work won over his co-stars, who were impressed with how deeply he got into his character, especially in the more emotional scenes. He knew intuitively how to listen and react to the other actors in a scene, but he wasn't sure what to do with his hands, which fluttered just below the frame when he wasn't using them or holding a prop. Compared with the film's top-billed stars, Richard Egan and Debra Paget, Presley had few scenes to shoot, but he did double-duty on the picture, going back and forth between the set and the recording studio, where he worked on the soundtrack recording. Presley had a busy promotional schedule as well, including an appearance on *The Ed Sullivan Show* to sing "Love Me Tender" two weeks before the film's release.

Marketing and promotion of Presley's role in *Love Me Tender* was heavy, and the film was even renamed from its original title, *The Reno Brothers,* to connect it with the Presley single. *Love Me Tender* had a sensational premiere in New York City in November 1956, with hundreds of teenagers, and a few truant officers, assembled outside the Times Square Theatre by 8:00 a.m. When it opened nationally a week later, *Love Me Tender* quickly became the number two film in the country, behind the James Dean epic *Giant* (1956). In response to the heavy marketing of the film to teen audiences, reviews focused on *Love Me Tender* as a pop culture phenomenon

> "It's about time somebody opened your eyes, kid. He wanted her. And now he's run away with her."
>
> — Mike Gavin (Neville Brand) to Clint Reno (Presley)

Clint excites the festival crowd with his rousing rendition of "Let Me Be."

and tended to ignore the film's dramatic elements, high production values, and talented cast. "Is it a sausage?" asked a *Time* magazine review sarcastically, referring to the packaging of Presley. A review in *The Reporter* attempted to explain the cultural significance of Presley's film debut with a biting analysis that concluded, "The new hero is an adolescent. Whether he is twenty or thirty or forty, he is fifteen and excessively sorry for himself. He is essentially a lone wolf who wants to belong."

Today, without the din of the studio's hype, the film can now be enjoyed on it merits, which are many. There was nothing manufactured about the enthusiasm and energy Presley brought to the project, and those natural qualities make *Love Me Tender* one of the best films of his long career.

SONGS IN LOVE ME TENDER

"Love Me Tender"

"Let Me Be"

"Poor Boy"

"We're Gonna Move"

Top: Vance Reno's gang boards the train car to rescue their leader from the authorities. Bottom: Cathy gives Vance the money he needs to secure his freedom.

LOVING YOU (1957)

PARAMOUNT PICTURES

DIRECTOR: HAL KANTER

SCREENPLAY: HAL KANTER AND HERBERT BAKER

PRINCIPAL CAST: ELVIS PRESLEY (DEKE RIVERS), LIZABETH SCOTT (GLENDA MARKLE), WENDELL COREY (WALTER "TEX" WARNER), DOLORES HART (SUSAN JESSUP) AND JAMES GLEASON (CARL MEADE)

With *Loving You*, Elvis Presley's second feature film, expectations were distinctly divided. On one side was Presley's manager, Colonel Tom Parker, who had teamed up with veteran film producer Hal Wallis to erase Presley's bad-boy image and position him for a long career in family-friendly films, the type of entertainment that would draw audiences long after the rock and roll craze had faded. At the same time, Presley and his fans had something else in mind; they wanted him to be the new James Dean.

Loving You is a showcase for Presley's talents onstage, an attempt to capture on-screen the excitement he generated in television and live concert performances. Presley plays Deke Rivers, a small-town beer delivery man who stumbles into a traveling honky-tonk show in the town square and gets pulled on stage to provide some local flavor. The show's promoter, Glenda Markle (Lizabeth Scott), sees the way girls in the audience respond to Deke,

Top: Music promoter Glenda Markle (Lizabeth Scott) sees star potential in beer delivery man Deke Rivers (Presley). Bottom: After watching Deke perform, Tex (Wendell Corey) and Glenda think they've found a surefire gimmick.

Top: Deke wows the small-town crowd. Bottom: Deke literally gets his moment in the spotlight.

and she offers him the chance to join the group, where he quickly becomes the main attraction on their roadshow tour. The group's leader, Tex Warner (Wendell Corey), doesn't mind the arrangement: the gigs keep getting bigger and the band members like Deke, who's always gracious and good-natured. Susan Jessup (Dolores Hart), the girl singer who formerly fronted the band, becomes Deke's love interest, and she's so supportive of the rising star that she doesn't mind a bit when she's booted from the group.

Deke starts out performing in blue jeans and moves up to silk cowboy outfits, but he stays grounded and morally upright, despite the trappings of fame: crowds of screaming girls waiting in front of the theater, smaller mobs pressing against the stage door, and the occasional vixen venturing backstage. Along the way, the once lonely Deke finds true friendship with the band and elevates all of them to a level of success they had long sought. Mostly, however, he sings, frequently launching into his trademark hip swivel and amazing the young while baffling the old.

The generational divide over rock and roll is a minor theme in *Loving You*, but unlike the popular rock and roll exploitation films of the time, featuring angry antagonists and a roster of defiant pop music stars, the conflict is portrayed as a difference in taste, not a cultural clash. When Deke performs at a Lion's Club jamboree, for example, teenagers squeal while the grown-ups scratch their heads. Later, when Deke cuts loose with an impromptu performance in a restaurant, the young crowd goes wild while the elderly proprietor just stands to the side and stares. He may wear his collar up, mumble song lyrics, and drag his leg on stage, but Deke is a still a good kid, the film tells us, and by extension, Presley is too.

To bring out the best of Presley on-screen, director Hal Kanter went to Memphis to get acquainted with him before filming began. Presley

Deke tears it up for a restaurant crowd.

invited the director to his home and impressed upon him his wish to be taken seriously as an actor, even reciting for Kanter a General Douglas MacArthur speech from memory. He explained to Kanter his observation that stars with lasting power, like James Dean, didn't smile on-screen; Presley therefore thought that he should refrain from smiling as well. Only mildly impressed, Kanter was nevertheless bowled over when they drove to Shreveport together so that Presley could appear on *The Louisiana Hayride*, a live radio showcase that had provided him his early breaks and made him a regional sensation. After experiencing the audience's reaction first-hand — screaming so loud that the songs could not be heard — Kanter returned to Hollywood to rewrite the *Loving You* script. The veteran comedy writer turned filmmaker wanted to capture the excitement of Presley's live appearances on-screen in the rock and roll idol's second film.

Presley spent the first two months of 1957 in Los Angeles working on *Loving You*, alternating his time between the soundstages at Paramount and recording sessions at a local studio. In the comfortable confines of the recording studio, he recorded an EP of gospel songs, the single "All Shook Up," and studio versions of

"It's not my future you care about, it's yours. It's what I can do for you. You don't care about me, or Tex, or about anybody but yourself."

— Deke Rivers (Presley) to Glenda Markle (Lizabeth Scott)

the songs for *Loving You* to ensure that there were safety tracks in case the recordings at Paramount fell flat. In fact, music recordings at the film studio proved difficult and unproductive, since the setting was a large soundstage where curious actors and studio staff were free to wander in and take a look. In the end, many of the songs featured in the film were taken from the off-site sessions.

Loving You opened in July 1957 and quickly became a national hit, eventually ranking as one of the top-grossing films of the year and one of the biggest in Presley's film career. There was a long-term payoff as well: by suggesting that he and his screen character were one and the same, Presley's image was effectively sanitized. Even *Time* magazine took the bait, referring to *Loving You* as an "authorized pseudo biography" and noting that "the only substantial departure from fact is that the movie's Deke Rivers is a clean-living Texas orphan, whereas Elvis is actually a clean-living Tennessee homebody with a real mom and pop."

The careful planning that went into *Loving You* works beautifully in the final product, now regarded as a pop culture landmark that has influenced rock and roll films for decades. Sadly, the idea of Presley as a film artist, holding his own alongside great Method actors of the day, was a notion that quickly faded away. The plot of *Loving You* — the working-class singer lifted from obscurity by an opportunist agent, fending off bullies and sexually inappropriate women — became the Presley film template. Many fans believed his skill as an actor was yet untapped, but they were willing to line up, over and over, for more of the Presley they already knew and loved.

Top: Deke settles a score with a local bully (Ken Becker). Bottom: From the wings, Susan (Dolores Hart) and Carl (James Gleason) watch Deke bring down the house.

At her family's farm, Susan spends quiet time with Deke before he heads back out on the road.

Songs in Loving You

"Let Me Be Your Teddy Bear"

"Got a Lot of Livin' to Do"

"Loving You"

"Lonesome Cowboy"

"Hot Dog"

"Mean Woman Blues"

"Let's Have a Party"

"They make it sound like that folks oughta be ashamed just listening to me sing."

— Deke Rivers (Presley) to Glenda Markle (Lizabeth Scott)

JAILHOUSE ROCK (1957)

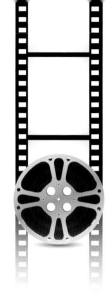

MGM

DIRECTOR: RICHARD THORPE

SCREENPLAY: GUY TROSPER

PRINCIPAL CAST: ELVIS PRESLEY (VINCE EVERETT), JUDY TYLER (PEGGY VAN ALDEN), MICKEY SHAUGHNESSY (HUNK HOUGHTON), VAUGHN TAYLOR (MR. SHORES) AND DEAN JONES (TEDDY TALBOT)

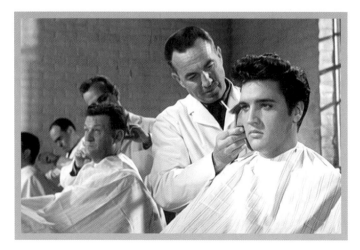

Tapping into a youth culture that was rapidly becoming an important audience for *all* forms of entertainment media, Hollywood embraced Elvis Presley, even if they didn't quite understand him. Was he a rock and roll hellion in the mold of Marlon Brando and James Dean, inciting teens to reject parental authority? Or was the church-going, gospel music–loving Presley "a real decent, fine boy" in the words of television host Ed Sullivan? The trick for Hollywood was mixing the right public-image elements to create a film that was both a little shocking and enormously entertaining. With *Jailhouse Rock*, they hit the mark.

In the role of Vince Everett, Presley comes across as far less menacing than other popular film rebels of the era, like Marlon Brando's biker antihero in *The Wild One* (1953), but he's hard-edged and eager to offend. Within minutes of the film's opening, Vince accidentally kills a man in a bar fight; a few short scenes later he's behind

Top: Hunk Houghton (Mickey Shaughnessy) explains the inmates' code to his new cell mate, Vince Everett (Presley). Bottom: The price of crime: Vince loses his pompadour with his first prison haircut.

bars, calmly strumming a guitar. By chance Vince's cell mate Hunk Houghton (Mickey Shaughnessy) is running the joint; seeing musical promise in the young "Sonny Buck," Hunk arranges for Vince to make his debut on a televised prison musical show — and cons him into signing away half his future earnings.

On the outside, Vince meets Peggy Van Alden (Judy Tyler), a young socialite with experience in the record business. With Peggy's help, Vince quickly becomes a major star, appearing on television to gyrate through an elaborate "Jailhouse Rock" production number and signing a Hollywood contract. Stardom does little to quell Vince's antisocial tendencies; in fact, he becomes even more surly and arrogant, alienating Peggy and others in his circle, until a brutal fight paves the way for his redemption.

The brutish nature of Presley's character in *Jailhouse Rock* runs contrary to his reputation as sweet-natured and polite (at least in the early days of his career). But many aspects of the story mirror the life Presley was leading at that time, and not always in a flattering sense. An early scene in which Vince signs away half his earnings to a rotund conniver seems eerily close to stories about his earliest management deals; the small-time studio in which Vince cuts his first record is an almost-perfect replica of Sun Studios, where the teenaged Presley laid down his very first tracks; and Vince's friends evolve into an entourage-on-the-payroll, like his famous "Memphis

Top: At the prisoners showcase, Vince is a hit with his rendition of "I Want to Be Free." Bottom: In his rented room, ex-con Vince reads his first fan letter.

Mafia" crew. Finally, Vince's first feature film, a quickly made vehicle for a pop singer who's still learning his craft, almost appears to be a spoof on *Jailhouse Rock* itself.

Unlike his *Jailhouse Rock* alter ego, however, Presley didn't spend his days reveling in the perks of stardom; he was too busy working at a furious pace to maximize his commercial potential.

Rushing from television soundstage to film set to recording studio, Presley starred in three films in a 12-month period, made countless public appearances, and recorded so frequently that his fans only had to wait a matter of weeks for new material. Case in point: Presley released both a "Jailhouse Rock" single *and* an EP before the film was even released.

The outstanding songs in *Jailhouse Rock,* primarily written by the pop hit makers Jerry Leiber and Mike Stoller, provide Presley with the best possible material and elevate the film above standard teen movie fare, as does the first-rate cast.

In a dive bar, Vince barely gets noticed when he croons "Young and Beautiful."

"That ain't tactics, honey. It's just the beast in me"

— Vince Everett (Presley) to Peggy Van Alden (Judy Tyler)

"I'm an animal in a jungle, and I got a motto: Do unto others as they would do unto you — only do it first."

— Hunk Houghton (Mickey Shaughnessy) to Vince Everett (Presley)

Top: A partnership begins when Peggy Van Alden (Judy Tyler) offers her help to a discouraged Vince. Bottom: Vince cuts his first record in a $20 recording session.

Portraying Vince's wheeler-dealer cell mate Hunk, Shaughnessy gives the strongest performance in *Jailhouse Rock;* the scene where Hunk outlines the convict's code is one of the film's highlights. Dean Jones — looking only slightly more youthful than when he starred in Disney's *The Love Bug* (1969) — is solid as the helpful disc jockey Teddy Talbot. Presley's actual back-up band, including guitarist Scotty Moore and bass player Bill Black, play the wordless studio musicians who become part of Vince's crew. And Judy Tyler, formerly a child actor on the *Howdy Doody* television show, skillfully handles the role of Peggy Van Alden, the business partner and love interest who helps launch Vince's career. Tragically, she would never make another film again; just days after finishing *Jailhouse Rock*, Tyler was killed in a car wreck. The news of her death reportedly devastated Presley, who was widely quoted as saying he would never be able to watch the finished film.

DJ Teddy Talbot (Dean Jones) gives Vince's record a spin.

Jailhouse Rock was a hit with young audiences, who quickly made it one of the highest-grossing films of the year. It hardly mattered to Presley fans that *Variety*'s critic faulted the film for its "contrived plot." *Jailhouse Rock* was also a smash in Europe, where teens worshiped Presley as the American rebel ideal. In Italy, the film was retitled *Il delinquente del Rock and Roll (The Delinquent of Rock and Roll)*.

Selected for preservation by the National Film Registry as a "culturally, historically or aesthetically significant film" in 2004, *Jailhouse Rock* features one of Presley's most magnetic screen performances. The MGM film also captures the 22-year-old superstar at a turning point in his life and career. Although Presley had tried to remain accessible and open to the public, especially in his adopted hometown of Memphis, Tennessee, those days were coming to an end.

Vince Everett signs copies of his first hit single for fans at a local record shop.

"You look sexy tonight — start the hammers to pounding in my skull."

— Vince Everett (Presley) to Peggy Van Alden (Judy Tyler)

While filming *Jailhouse Rock*, he bought the Memphis mansion Graceland and promptly called in architects to make improvements to the property: a soda fountain, a swimming pool, and iron gates to keep the fans away.

Vince shows Peggy his new cuff links — the mark of a man's success.

"Emotion? What emotion? It's strictly business between you and me."

— Vince Everett (Presley) to Peggy Van Alden (Judy Tyler)

SONGS FROM JAILHOUSE ROCK

"Jailhouse Rock"

"Treat Me Nice"

"Young and Beautiful"

"I Wanna Be Free"

"Don't Leave Me Now"

"Baby, I Don't Care"

"One More Day"

Top: Presley performs the film's title track, one of his most popular songs. Bottom: Now a movie star, Vince celebrates his success with a rousing, poolside rendition of "Baby, I Don't Care."

KING CREOLE (1958)

PARAMOUNT PICTURES

DIRECTOR: MICHAEL CURTIZ

SCREENPLAY: HERBERT BAKER AND MICHAEL V. GAZZO

BASED ON THE NOVEL "A STONE FOR DANNY FISHER" BY HAROLD ROBBINS

PRINCIPAL CAST: ELVIS PRESLEY (DANNY FISHER), CAROLYN JONES (RONNIE), WALTER MATTHAU (MAXIE FIELDS), DOLORES HART (NELLIE), DEAN JAGGER (MR. FISHER), JAN SHEPARD (MIMI), VIC MORROW (SHARK) AND PAUL STEWART (CHARLIE LE GRAND)

Of the 31 feature films Elvis Presley made between 1956 and 1969, *King Creole* ranks as one of the rock and roll legend's finest achievements on celluloid. A loose adaptation of Harold Robbins' 1952 best-selling novel *A Stone for Danny Fisher*, this finely etched portrait of a singer caught up in the New Orleans underworld has an emotional heft that's conspicuously lacking from most of Presley's films.

Adapted for the screen by screenwriter Herbert Baker and actor/playwright Michael V. Gazzo (*A Hatful of Rain*), *King Creole* takes considerable dramatic liberties with its source material; a promising boxer in Robbins' Bronx-set novel, Danny becomes an aspiring singer in Michael Curtiz's film, which unfolds against the colorful backdrop of New Orleans' French Quarter. Otherwise, *King Creole* faithfully captures the seedy atmosphere Robbins describes in his typically hard-hitting, often sexually graphic prose.

Top: Danny Fisher (Presley) consoles his sister Mimi (Jan Shepard). Bottom: Presley gives the finest dramatic performance of his career in *King Creole*.

In a role once intended for James Dean, Presley portrays Danny, a rebellious but basically kind-hearted young man who's flunked out of high school, in part because he's working to support his unemployed father (veteran character actor Dean Jagger). Danny briefly turns to petty theft but vows to go straight once he meets fresh-faced Nellie (Dolores Hart) and lands a singing gig at the King Creole saloon. Just when everything seems to be turning around for Danny, his criminal past comes back to haunt him in the form of local mob boss Maxie Fields (Walter Matthau). Eager to capitalize on Danny's growing fame, Maxie effectively orders Danny to sing at *his* nightclub, The Blue Shade. Although Danny wants to steer clear of Maxie, he finds himself drawn ever deeper into the gangster's world, thanks to his involvement with Ronnie (Carolyn Jones), Maxie's erstwhile mistress.

Landing the role of Danny was a coup for Presley; besides Dean, Marlon Brando, Tony Curtis, Ben Gazzara and Paul Newman were reportedly considered for the part when it more closely resembled Robbins' character. Casting Presley as a Bronx boxer would have strained credulity past the proverbial breaking point, so it was a shrewd decision on the filmmakers' part to tailor the role to Presley's strengths. The songs, including three by Presley's *Jailhouse Rock* songwriting team Jerry Leiber and Mike Stoller, are smoothly integrated into the narrative and showcase Presley to spectacular advantage, particularly his blues-infected rendition of Leiber and Stoller's "Trouble," one of the film's musical highlights.

Top: "So would you like to hang out with us?" Danny Fisher with Shark (Vic Morrow), a New Orleans hoodlum. Bottom: A tense moment between Danny and his father (Dean Jagger).

Walter Matthau excels as New Orleans mobster Maxie Fields in *King Creole*. Opposite page: The hoodlum turned singing sensation heats up the joint.

Although the filmmakers toned down the more sordid elements of Robbins' novel, it took years for the Motion Picture Production Code Administration to grant begrudging approval to the *King Creole* screenplay; Hollywood's morality watchdogs objected to the screenplay's depiction of a seamy French Quarter awash in sex and crime. Nor did the film's soundtrack escape the censors' notice; they especially balked at the "suggestive and vulgar" lyrics to the song "Banana," sung by stripper Forty Nina (Liliane Montevecchi). Leiber and Stoller were also forced to change the name of their song "I'm Evil" to "Trouble."

Happily, the filmmakers' struggles with the Production Code did not cast a pall over *King Creole*. One of the most versatile directors of Hollywood's golden age, Curtiz was a prolific and autocratic Hollywood veteran whose films ran the gamut from *The Adventures of Robin Hood* (1938) to *Casablanca* (1943). Taking over the directorial reins of *King Creole* from Sidney Lumet, Curtiz brings his keen feel for character and mood to Presley's fourth film. Under his customarily assured

"I guess there's a last time for everything."

— Danny Fisher (Presley)

direction, *King Creole* calls to mind a 1940s-era noir; indeed, the shadowy nightclubs and streets of New Orleans lend the film an authentic grit. In the words of film critic/historian Gerald Peary, "For once, Elvis had a real director."

Not one to suffer fools or temperamental stars gladly — he had kept Warner Bros. diva Joan Crawford in line in two films, *Mildred Pierce* (1945) and *Flamingo Road* (1949) — Curtiz had approved Presley's casting and worked patiently with the inexperienced actor. Presley, who obtained a draft extension to complete the film before going into the army, rose to the challenge of playing Danny, who bears more than a passing resemblance to Dean's *Rebel Without a Cause* (1955) antihero Jim Stark in his raw anger and emotional vulnerability.

Curtiz also surrounded Presley with a cast of truly fine actors, including his talented *Loving You* (1957) co-star Hart, Jagger, Jones and Matthau, then just beginning his decades-long career as one of Hollywood's most reliable and likable character actors. Nearly 30 years after he shared the screen with Presley, Matthau would sing the rock and roll legend's praises in a 1987 interview, calling him "an instinctive actor … very elegant, sedate, and refined, and sophisticated."

"You do something wrong and that makes you do something worse, and the next thing you know, you don't know the difference anymore."

— Ronnie (Carolyn Jones) on what will happen to Danny Fisher (Presley)

SONGS IN
KING CREOLE

"King Creole"

"As Long as I Have You"

"Hard Headed Woman"

"Trouble"

"Dixieland Rock"

"Don't Ask Me Why"

"Lover Doll"

"Crawfish"

"Young Dreams"

"Steadfast, Loyal and True"

"New Orleans"

"Turtles"

"Berries and Gumbo"

"Banana"

Top: Danny's behavior
leaves Nellie (Dolores Hart)
heartbroken. Bottom: Charles
Le Grand (Paul Stewart) speaks
with Danny about the tough
decision he faces.

Despite some story contrivances and structural flaws, *King Creole* received good reviews, and a number of critics commended Presley for his performance. *Variety* found Presley "surprisingly sympathetic and believable on occasion." *The Los Angeles Times* remarked, "Elvis is the surprise of the day. He delivers his lines with good comic timing, considerable intelligence and even flashes of sensitivity. If he's been studying, it's paying off handsomely." *Daily Variety* called the film "the best film showcase the young singer has yet had." Even the *New York Times* proclaimed "Elvis Presley can act."

In *King Creole*, the camera loves Presley. The 23-year-old star smolders on the screen in what is arguably the sexiest performance of his career. His *Loving You* co-star Lizabeth Scott summed up Presley's magnetism when she observed that "his eyes were just so powerful in the sense of being sexy, piercing, playful."

Given the positive reviews Presley received for *King Creole*, it's therefore all the more dispiriting that he never tackled another role as demanding and multi-faceted as Danny Fisher. Nor would he ever work with another director as gifted as Curtiz, who had helped the acting novice realize his dramatic potential. But as Presley historian Alan Hanson so aptly puts it, "At least we have *King Creole* to remind us of what might have been."

"I guess there's a last time for everything." Danny confides his feelings to Nellie.

"Elvis Presley can act."

— Howard Thompson, *New York Times* review of *King Creole*

PART 2

1960-1964

ELVIS PRESLEY: 1960-1964

Two weeks before he was officially discharged from the U.S. Army, Presley gave his only interview to the military's official newspaper, *Stars and Stripes*. Although he had not been in a recording studio or on a Hollywood soundstage for two years, Presley was still *the* teen idol for his fans, who clamored for every scrap of news, no matter how trivial, about the 25-year-old. No longer decried as the hip-swiveling symbol of the nation's imminent downfall, "Elvis the Pelvis" had become one of the most "bankable" stars in Hollywood — a box office draw who appealed to all generations of filmgoers.

Yet when *Stars and Stripes* staff writer Wally Beene interviewed Presley, the rock and roll idol came across as disarmingly humble and full of nervous energy. There was no hint of entitlement or ego in Presley, who habitually bit his nails and tapped his foot. Conscious that any slip-up would generate gossip and criticism, Presley had been a model soldier during his 18 months of military service. Stationed in Friedberg, Germany, he had

PRESLEY'S LEADING LADIES, 1960-1964

ANN-MARGRET
Viva Las Vegas (1964)

Billed as the "female Elvis," the Swedish-born actress/dancer/singer was hot off the success of *Bye Bye Birdie* (1963) when she teamed with Presley for *Viva Las Vegas* (1964). Working at a furious pace throughout the 1960s, she only achieved critical respect with her Academy Award–nominated performance as a vulnerable, aging party girl in *Carnal Knowledge* (1971). Ann-Margret later won raves for her Emmy-nominated performance as Blanche Du Bois in a television version of *A Streetcar Named Desire* (1984).

URSULA ANDRESS
Fun in Acapulco (1963)

Rising out of the Caribbean surf in a white bikini, Andress earned her place in film history as the first Bond girl in *Doctor No* (1962). Called "the most awesome piece of natural Swiss architecture since the Alps," the statuesque beauty parlayed her 007 fame into starring roles in films ranging from *What's New, Pussycat?* (1965) to *The Clash of the Titans* (1981). Andress also spoofed her Bond girl image in the first, tongue-in-cheek version of Ian Fleming's *Casino Royale* (1967).

BARBARA EDEN
Flaming Star (1960)

Eden made several feature films, including *Voyage to the Bottom of the Sea* (1961) and *The Wonderful World of the Brothers Grimm* (1962), before finding her niche in the sitcom *I Dream of Jeannie*. The NBC sitcom ran for five seasons (1965–1970) and continues to play in syndication. A ubiquitous presence on the small screen, Eden later starred in the short-lived sitcom *Harper Valley PTA*, which aired on NBC from 1981 to 1982.

performed his assigned duties without complaint. He served first as jeep driver and was eventually promoted to sergeant in command of a three-man reconnaissance team for the Third Armored Division's 32nd Scout Platoon. While some charged that he received special treatment, the only luxury granted Presley was permission to live off post with his father and his grandmother. Presley was formally discharged March 5, 1960.

Thanks largely to manager Colonel Tom Parker's media manipulations, Presley's fans had remained loyal and greeted his return with predictable hysteria. Between 1958 and 1960, with its top star stationed overseas, RCA Victor had faced a dearth of new material. At Parker's behest, Victor repackaged and re-released previous Elvis recordings, keeping Presley on the charts and selling millions of records even in absentia. In the meantime, the face of rock and roll had changed: Jerry Lee Lewis had been banished from the public sphere in the wake of scandal; the industry was under investigation for payola; and the chart-toppers of 1959 were all Presley imitators — Ricky Nelson, Fabian, Frankie Avalon and Bobby Darin. Presley's fans were slavering for his return.

HOPE LANGE
Wild in the Country (1961)

Elegant and sophisticated, Lange began her career as a child actress on Broadway in the 1940s. After making her feature film debut in *Bus Stop* (1956), she received a Best Supporting Actress nomination for her sensitive performance in *Peyton Place* (1957). A slew of juicy roles followed, including leads in *The Best of Everything* (1959) and Frank Capra's last film, *Pocketful of Miracles* (1961). She won consecutive Emmy Awards for the NBC sitcom *The Ghost and Mrs. Muir,* which ran from 1968 to 1970.

JULIET PROWSE
G.I. Blues (1960)

Reportedly discovered by choreographer Hermes Pan, Fred Astaire's longtime collaborator, Prowse made international headlines when Soviet leader Nikita Khrushchev pronounced her dancing in *Can-Can* (1960) "immoral." Despite the press attention, the South African–raised, classically trained dancer only found sporadic work in Hollywood, where she made a handful of films besides *Can-Can* and *G.I. Blues*. Prowse later became a star headliner in Las Vegas and a television pitchwoman for L'eggs pantyhose.

TUESDAY WELD
Wild in the Country (1961)

Named the Most Promising Female Newcomer by the Hollywood Foreign Press Association in 1960, Weld made good on that award by giving critically lauded performances in such films as *The Cincinnati Kid* (1965), *Lord Love a Duck* (1966) and the black comedy *Pretty Poison* (1968), in which she portrays a sociopathic high school girl on a murder spree. Very much in demand in the 1960s, Weld turned down starring roles in *Bonnie and Clyde* (1967), *Rosemary's Baby* (1968) and *Bob & Carol & Ted & Alice* (1969).

Oddly enough, Frank Sinatra would grant their wish. Only three years earlier, he had dismissed rock and rollers as "cretinous goons." Now Sinatra recognized the opportunity to boost ratings for his struggling series of television specials and agreed to pay Presley $125,000 for a six-minute appearance on his 1960 special — an unprecedented amount for the time. The gamble worked and earned *Frank Sinatra's Welcome Home Party for Elvis Presley* a whopping 41.5 Nielsen ratings share, steamrolling the competition.

Afterward, Presley appeared at various charitable events, including his famous concert at Pearl Harbor to help raise funds for the USS *Arizona* memorial. Colonel Parker, however, seemed to have a new promotional strategy in mind for "his boy." Rather than indulge fans with personal appearances, Parker withdrew Presley from the public sphere. The Pearl Harbor concert would be Presley's last live performance for another eight years. Instead, Presley was to focus on his film career, and fans would have to pay to see their hero on the silver screen. The move, perhaps calculated to enhance Presley's mystique and "godlike" stature, wound up only frustrating the young performer.

"What do I do? Kiss you or salute you?"

— Presley, greeting his old friend from Sun Records, Marion Keisker, a WAF captain stationed in Germany

Presley strikes a patriotic pose in *G.I. Blues'* big finale, "Didya Ever."

Presley perfroms "Rock-A-Hula Baby" in *Blue Hawaii* (1961).

After the critical high point of *King Creole* (1958), Presley found himself stuck in a series of formulaic and derivative movies that did little to prove his talent or worth as an actor. Increasingly, the movies were cranked out in assembly-line fashion, with two-week shooting schedules. Most served as flimsy excuses for soundtrack albums, which continued to be hits, despite a discernible shift from Presley's early rock and roll to more adult contemporary fare. Regardless of the low quality of some of his films, Presley earned a place among Hollywood's elite million-dollar earners, and even took in 50 percent of each film's profits.

By this time, Presley's personal life was overshadowing his career. Rumors abounded of an affair between Presley and his *Viva Las Vegas* (1964) co-star Ann-Margret. Presley biographer Jerry Hopkins, however, called most of this a "publicist's puffery." The young woman who had caught Presley's eye back in Germany was Priscilla Ann Beaulieu, the stepdaughter of an air force major. In 1963, Beaulieu moved to Graceland and completed high school in Memphis. After graduation, she would make several trips to Hollywood to visit Presley at his new Los Angeles home, and it wouldn't be long before the King would decide it was time to settle down.

G.I. BLUES (1960)

PARAMOUNT PICTURES

DIRECTOR: NORMAN TAUROG

SCREENPLAY: EDMUND BELOIN AND HENRY GARSON

PRINCIPAL CAST: ELVIS PRESLEY (TULSA MCLEAN), JULIET PROWSE (LILI),
ROBERT IVERS (COOKIE), JAMES DOUGLAS (RICK), ARCH JOHNSON
(SERGEANT MCGRAW), JEREMY SLATE (TURK), LETÍCIA ROMÁN (TINA) AND
SIGRID MAIER (MARLA)

The first musical *comedy* Presley ever made, the highly anticipated *G.I. Blues* (1960), drew long lines of adoring fans, eager to see their idol back on the big screen after a two-year absence. It was also now the only way to see Presley perform, since he was taking an extended break from live performing. As a result, *G.I. Blues* is chock-full of songs, most of which Presley reportedly complained weren't worth "a cat's ass." But either Presley lost his sense of what was musically good while he was in the army or the public was so starved for new music from him that *they* lost perspective, because the *G.I. Blues* soundtrack LP reached number one on the *Billboard* pop chart and earned a Grammy nomination.

Admittedly, the songs in *G.I. Blues* do not rank among Presley's finest. Nor did any of these songs become jukebox hits, save for "Wooden Heart," which topped the pop charts in Europe. Whatever their musical

Top: Tulsa (Presley) inside a tank. In real life, Presley was assigned to the Third Armored Division, stationed in West Germany as part of the NATO forces. Bottom: Presley's shower scene in *G.I. Blues* was a hit with his fans.

shortcomings, the film's songs are nevertheless diverting and occasionally catchy, especially the title track and the upbeat "Frankfurt Special." The latter, which Presley performs with customary showmanship in a sequence set aboard a train, inspired a good-natured parody in the spy spoof *Top Secret!* (1984).

As for the film itself, *G.I. Blues* represents a distinct letdown after *King Creole* (1958). Originally titled *Café Europa*, Presley's fifth film uses a narrative hook reminiscent of the setup in the Broadway musical *Guys and Dolls*: the hero makes a wager that he can win over a frosty beauty. In *G.I. Blues*, army specialist Tulsa McLean (Presley) and his buddies Cookie (Robert Ivers) and Rick (James Douglas) dream of starting a nightclub once they complete their military service in West Germany. With little in the way of seed money, however, they pool their meager resources to bet on an army friend, "Dynamite" (Edward Stroll), who's got a wager going with ladies' man Turk (Jeremy Slate) that he can spend the whole night with Lili (Juliet Prowse), an aloof dancer in a Frankfurt cabaret. When Dynamite gets transferred before the contest begins, Tulsa agrees to take his place and launches a major charm offensive against Lili. What began as a wager gradually turns into a romance — a development that prompts a crisis of conscience for Tulsa. Should he tell Lili the truth and risk losing his dream of starting a nightclub? Or follow through on the bet and risk losing her?

Filming in Germany began even before Presley was discharged, with a Mississippian by the name of Tom

Top: Tulsa and his buddies perform in a West German club. Bottom: Tulsa puts the moves on Lili (Juliet Prowse).

47

Tulsa with Sergeant McGraw (Arch Johnson).

Creel serving as his stand-in. According to one of Presley's army buddies who snagged a part as an extra, the German girls frequently mistook Creel for Elvis, so the stand-in signed autographs for them. When Presley did join the production, the *G.I. Blues* set became a magnet for royalty, with visits from Scandinavian princesses and Thailand's ruling couple. Most of *G.I. Blues* was ultimately filmed in Hollywood, using process-screen shots, rather than footage of Presley and his co-stars on location.

Shooting in Hollywood may have been convenient and economical, but it threw a crimp in Presley's dalliance with Prowse, the leggy South African dancer who had wowed audiences in *Can-Can* (1960). Although engaged to Frank Sinatra, Prowse embarked on an affair with Presley. According to Presley's "Memphis Mafia" crony Red West, the *G.I. Blues* stars spent so much time together in a trailer that West once played a joke on them, shouting "Frank's coming!" Bodyguards in tow, Sinatra later made an impromptu visit to the set and discovered Presley and Prowse together — rehearsing lines.

"I'm so pleased you came to Germany. I'm going to write a thank-you letter to your draft board."

— Lili (Juliet Prowse)

One of Presley's most dynamic co-stars, Prowse imbues Lili with grace and sizzling sensuality; she nearly succeeds in stealing the spotlight from Presley, who comes across as amiable and relaxed in his first big-screen comedy. Gone is the brooding, chip-on-his-shoulder persona he had cultivated in his previous films. In *G.I. Blues*, Presley is likable and shows a natural flair for comedy. If Norman Taurog's film is innocuous to the point of being forgettable, it's still an engaging showcase for Presley.

Critics were underwhelmed by Presley's much-ballyhooed return to the big screen. Although *Variety* complained that "the creakiest 'book' in musical comedy annals has been revived by the scenarists as a framework within which Elvis Presley warbles 10 wobbly songs," *G.I. Blues* became the fourteenth highest grossing film of the year at $4.3 million.

SONGS IN G.I. BLUES

"G.I. Blues"

"Tonight Is So Right for Love"

"Frankfurt Special"

"Wooden Heart"

"Pocketful of Rainbows"

"Didya Ever?"

"What's She Really Like?"

"Shoppin' Around"

"Big Boots"

"Doin' the Best I Can"

Top: Tulsa shares the spotlight with a puppet while singing "Wooden Heart." Bottom: Mission accomplished: Tulsa and Lili fall in love.

FLAMING STAR (1960)

TWENTIETH CENTURY FOX

DIRECTOR: DON SIEGEL

SCREENPLAY: NUNNALLY JOHNSON AND CLAIR HUFFAKER

BASED ON THE NOVEL "FLAMING LANCE" BY HUFFAKER

PRINCIPAL CAST: ELVIS PRESLEY (PACER BURTON), STEVE FORREST (CLINT BURTON), BARBARA EDEN (ROSLYN PIERCE), DOLORES DEL RIO (NEDDY BURTON), RUDOLPH ACOSTA (BUFFALO HORN) AND JOHN MCINTIRE (SAM BURTON)

To any other actor in Hollywood, *Flaming Star* might have been just another genre picture, albeit one with serious themes concerning race and identity. But to Presley, Don Siegel's western drama represented a chance to escape the steady diet of lightweight musicals his manager Colonel Tom Parker had prescribed as the key to box office success and superstardom on the big screen. Stepping into a part once earmarked for Marlon Brando, Presley saw *Flaming Star* as an opportunity to show everyone that he was more than just a swivel-hipped singing star — if only his fans would let him out of that musical straitjacket.

The drama opens on a familiar note: as Pacer Burton (Presley) entertains at a party, singing and playing guitar, Pacer's world is rocked when marauding Kiowa warriors murder family friends. Seeking revenge against the whites stealing Kiowa land, new chief Buffalo Horn (Rudolph Acosta) has declared war against the Burtons' neighbors.

Top: Pacer Burton (Elvis Presley) entertains family and friends in a happy moment before violence tears them apart. Bottom: Sam Burton (John McIntire) and sons Pacer and Clint (Steve Forrest) defend their family home.

Pacer, the son of a white father, Sam (John McIntire), and full-blooded Kiowa mother, Neddy (Dolores del Rio), is caught in the middle. The whites regard him with suspicion; even Roslyn (Barbara Eden), his half-brother Clint's (Steve Forrest) girlfriend, is skeptical of Pacer's loyalty to their small Texas community, despite their lifelong friendship. Buffalo Horn tries to recruit Pacer for his blood feud, but Pacer feels no sense of belonging in the native world either. As the war between the whites and the Kiowa heats up, Pacer and his kin are trapped between both sides.

No one will ever mistake *Flaming Star,* with its hackneyed dialogue, for one of the great westerns. Yet despite its flaws, Presley's sixth film is a satisfying entertainment, bracing and poignant. Siegel, who would go on to make five films with Clint Eastwood, including *Dirty Harry* (1971), is a master of his craft; he stages the action scenes for maximum impact. The fight scenes in *Flaming Star* have a visceral force that still pack a wallop, thanks to Siegel's assured direction.

The director also took much care in the handling of his leading man. When it came to *Flaming Star*'s physical action, Siegel had full confidence in his star's athletic prowess. In shooting one scene, Presley reportedly proved himself to be a faster and better fighter than his opponent, a stuntman with a black belt in karate.

Presley did not have as much confidence himself as an actor, especially when it came to one particularly

Top: Pacer visits his Kiowa kin in a last-ditch effort to prevent more bloodshed. Bottom: Pacer comes to the aid of his wounded mother, Neddy (Dolores del Rio).

emotional moment in the film. "Elvis felt that he couldn't do the scene; he felt his acting talent wasn't equal to the sequence. When I pointed out to him that we would rehearse until he was satisfied with his performance, he begged for more time to prepare," Siegel remembered. Presley was so panicked over it that he even offered to let his director drive his new Rolls-Royce if only Siegel would postpone the scene.

Siegel kept the car for two weeks, recalling, "When the inevitable time came to do the scene, I returned his Rolls-Royce. To Presley's amazement and mine, Elvis gave his finest performance ever."

In Siegel, Presley had a genuine champion on a movie in which he otherwise had precious little support. Nunnally Johnson, the Oscar-nominated screenwriter of *The Grapes of Wrath* (1940), adapted Clair Huffaker's novel expressly for Brando. When the script became a vehicle for Presley, Johnson quit the film, leaving Huffaker to deal with extensive rewrites.

The people ostensibly in Presley's corner were just as unsupportive. The studio and Colonel Parker wanted *Flaming Star* transformed into a full-blown, song-happy

Pacer takes Dottie Phillips (Barbara Beaird) hostage in a desperate attempt to lure the doctor to his mother's side.

"They ain't my people. To tell you the truth, I don't know who's my people."

— Pacer Burton (Presley) on his Kiowa kin

musical, defeating Presley's desire to stretch himself as an actor. A horrified Siegel insisted that the drama could not support more than two numbers, the title tune and the song Pacer sings at the party before the action is engaged. "How can Elvis sing 'rock' songs, or any other kind of songs after the traumatic experiences that constantly plague him?" Siegel argued.

"Presley surprised me with his sensitivity as an actor," Siegel observed. "Colonel Parker, his mentor and personal manager, thought there should definitely be more songs. He was wrong on two counts: Elvis could have become an acting star, not just a singing star; also, he would have been happier."

"Colonel Parker was strictly interested in the buck," Siegel added. But to be fair to Presley's manager, maybe it was just that he understood what the public expected from the heartthrob. *Flaming Star* opened during the holiday season in December 1960. Critic A.H. Weiler writing in the *New York Times* praised the film as "an unpretentious but sturdy Western that takes the time, the place, and the people seriously" and declared that Presley "is a passable red youth." *Variety* was not so kind. While declaring the movie "consistently entertaining," it also dismissed it as overly familiar and often unconvincing, adding, "The role is a demanding one for

"If it's going to be like this the rest of my life, then the hell with it. I been killed already. I'm just stubborn about dying."

— Pacer Burton (Presley)

As Roslyn Pierce (Barbara Eden) and Clint watch, an enraged Pacer threatens Doc Phillips (Ford Rainey).

Sam and son Pacer embrace in an emotional farewell.

Presley. But he lacks the facial and thespic sensitivity and projection so desperately required here."

The film tanked as Presley's fans and everyone else stayed away. In its first nine days of release, *Flaming Star* earned a paltry $900. Presley took on another dramatic role in his next film, the Clifford Odets–penned *Wild in the Country* (1961), but his flirtation with serious acting was at its end. Starting with *Blue Hawaii* (1961), the parade of light musical comedies so beloved by Colonel Parker and movie studio brass began. But time has proven Presley's instincts right as *Flaming Star*'s critical reputation has steadily risen. Both *Time Out* and critic David Thomson regard it as Presley's best film with Thomson offering that "[Presley] gives a genuine performance."

Calling Presley "surprisingly well-cast," critic Sean Axmaker sums up the star's appeal: "Don Siegel brings out [Presley's] character through body language and action, letting his angry silences and physical reactions carry his performance and his character. For the fans, he greases his hair back and flips up his collar for a few scenes and takes his shirt off in the third act, but otherwise the persona is absorbed into his character — his one song is essentially a family sing-along — for a quietly effective performance."

"I know I have a long way to go, but a man has to have a goal and acting's mine. The part I have in *Flaming Star* is the least like myself, but I would love to move on to new dramatic frontiers. I'm hoping in time to handle only straight roles."

— Presley

Top: An outnumbered Sam fights back against attacking Kiowa. Bottom: Clint gets the worst of it in battle, but stays in the saddle.

55

WILD IN THE COUNTRY (1961)

TWENTIETH CENTURY FOX

DIRECTOR: PHILIP DUNNE

SCREENPLAY: CLIFFORD ODETS

BASED ON THE NOVEL "THE LOST COUNTRY" BY J.R. SALAMANCA

PRINCIPAL CAST: ELVIS PRESLEY (GLENN TYLER), HOPE LANGE (IRENE SPERRY), TUESDAY WELD (NOREEN BRAXTON), MILLIE PERKINS (BETTY LEE), JOHN IRELAND (PHIL MACY) AND GARY LOCKWOOD (MACY)

Elvis Presley arrived on the Napa, California, set of *Wild in the Country* in early November 1960, just as *G.I. Blues* was being primed and promoted for its Thanksgiving release. (The soundtrack was already racing up the charts.) He was embarking on his second straight dramatic role, after *Flaming Star* (1960), but that movie wouldn't reach theaters until Christmas. So there was no sense yet of how the public would respond to Presley's admirable effort to prove he could not merely perform in front of the camera, but act.

Wild in the Country had a certain pedigree, with acclaimed playwright Clifford Odets adapting J.R. Salamanca's hefty, atmospheric 1958 novel *The Lost Country* for the screen. Fresh from winning the Best Actress Academy Award for *Room at the Top* (1959), French film star Simone Signoret was set to co-star

Top: At his parole hearing, country boy Glenn Tyler (Presley) and his no-good father (Harry Shannon) glare suspiciously at an inquisitive psychologist. Middle: Glenn and girlfriend Betty Lee (Millie Perkins) make small talk while the bored temptress Noreen (Tuesday Weld) strums her guitar. Bottom: Glenn Tyler's first session with therapist Irene Sperry (Hope Lange) gets off to an awkward start.

opposite Presley. Behind the camera was Philip Dunne, a prolific screenwriter who had parlayed that success into an undistinguished career as a director. His rarefied sensibility didn't mesh with Presley's spontaneity and raw energy, or perhaps Dunne was just tone deaf to his star's gifts and appeal. "I think I won a unique place in the directors' pantheon as the only director ever to make Elvis Presley listen to Bach," he wrote in his memoirs. "As a matter of fact, he loved it."

There's no way of verifying Dunne's boast, but his rather patronizing comment provides some insight as to why Dunne is unable to capture Presley's electricity on-screen. Millie Perkins, cast as Presley's character's girlfriend following her acclaimed debut in *The Diary of Anne Frank* (1959), said later, "I think that everybody making the movie thought, 'We're classier than all those other Elvis Presley movies. We're so much better.' Everyone was going around patting themselves on the back for being artists; they were going to do something with Elvis that other people couldn't, or didn't want to, do — and I think they didn't come up with the goods at all."

Presley plays Glenn Tyler, an unschooled Virginia country boy with no mother, a useless father, and a bad temper. After a night in the slammer for brawling, the scowling delinquent is sent to live with his uncle with the stipulation that he visit a psychologist every

Top: Glenn charms Betty Lee with "I Slipped, I Stumbled, I Fell." Middle: Glenn and Betty Lee resist the unfriendly overtures of Cliff Macy (Gary Lockwood) and his date Monica George (Christina Crawford). Bottom: Married businessman Phil Macy (John Ireland) mixes a late-afternoon martini for the woman he loves, Irene Sperry (Hope Lange).

Glenn serenades the tipsy
Noreen with "In My Way."

week. Presley's performance was meant to evoke the sensitive, misunderstood and impassioned rebels that James Dean and Marlon Brando had introduced to American films. In the early 1960s, Twentieth Century Fox was struggling to figure out how to capitalize on both the new "youth culture" and Presley's massive appeal, but one thing was certain: Dunne had little to no affinity for either Presley or "youth culture."

Wild in the Country gives Presley's character three love interests and four brief songs, a curious kind of New Math. While Perkins co-stars as Glenn's doe-eyed, straight-arrow girlfriend Betty Lee, Tuesday Weld plays her polar opposite: the white-trash temptress Noreen, who tries to seduce Glenn away from the virginal Betty Lee.

The central relationship in the movie, however, is between Glenn and the therapist Irene Sperry (Hope Lange). After a contentious introductory session, the suspicious, vulnerable young man gradually comes to accept the older woman as a skilled professional, even as a confidante. When she discovers and champions his writing talent — autobiographical prose, not rock and roll lyrics — Irene presents a world of previously unimagined possibilities for Glenn. She's opened the door to a life beyond two-bit jobs and a small town full of narrow-minded, mean-spirited people.

"Sympathy is never wasted, Betty Lee. One way or another, you get it back, or so it says in the Book."

— Glenn (Presley) to Betty Lee (Millie Perkins)

Taking over the role once intended for Signoret, Lange gives a solid, compassionate performance as the narrative's most mature character; unlike Betty Lee and Noreen, Irene is a woman with life experience. Then just 26 years old, Lange is fine, but she's simply too young for the role of a psychologist who functions as a mother surrogate to Glenn. The unsettling complexities of Irene and Glenn's May-December attraction are lost with Lange in the role, rather than the worldly and frankly middle-aged Signoret.

As Glenn, Presley eloquently conveys the character's earnestness, decency and confusion; he is never less than compulsively watchable, which only makes it all the more frustrating that *Wild in the Country* mostly fails to realize its dramatic potential.

Wild in the Country does not lend itself to musical interludes, but Colonel Parker knew they were essential for Presley's fans. So Presley and Lange sing a charming duet "Husky Dusky Day" in the car, while he makes the most of "I Slipped, I Stumbled, I Fell," "In My Way," and the title song. (Presley also recorded "Lonely Man" and "Forget Me Never" for the picture, but they weren't included.) His vocal performances supply some of the loveliest moments in *Wild in the Country*, even if the sequences don't fully fit with the logic of the film.

One of the strangest moments during production involved Christina Crawford, Joan Crawford's daughter, who has a tiny part in the film. She took exception to the way her boyfriend, a member of Presley's entourage, lit the star's

Top: Noreen kisses Glenn good-bye as she embarks on a new life. Bottom: Irene takes Glenn to the university library before meeting with a professor friend about the young man's future as a writing student.

"I think that everybody making the movie thought, 'We're classier than all those other Elvis Presley movies. We're so much better.' Everyone was going around patting themselves on the back for being artists; they were going to do something with Elvis that other people couldn't, or didn't want to, do—and I think they didn't come up with the goods at all."

— Millie Perkins

Songs from Wild in the Country

"I Slipped, I Stumbled, I Fell"

"In My Way"

"Wild in the Country"

"Husky Dusky Day"

Top: Glenn and Irene sing an a capella duet of "Husky Dusky Day." Bottom: Irene's professional ethics run afoul of her attraction to Glenn.

cigar. She slapped it out of Presley's mouth and he exploded, swearing at her and yanking her by the hair.

Torn between two lovers.

Wild in the Country opened in June 1961 to tepid reviews. "Dramatically, there simply isn't substance, novelty or spring to this wobbly and artificial tale," the trade paper *Variety* declared. However, it also noted, "Presley, subdued, uses what dramatic resources he has to best advantage in this film."

The box office receipts for *Wild in the Country* were respectable, but it was apparent that filmgoers preferred Presley singing and swiveling his way across the screen. He would not attempt to play such a challenging role as Glenn Tyler ever again.

"I think I won a unique place in the directors' pantheon as the only director ever to make Elvis Presley listen to Bach. As a matter of fact, he loved it."

— Philip Dunne

BLUE HAWAII (1961)

PARAMOUNT PICTURES

DIRECTOR: NORMAN TAUROG

SCREENPLAY: HAL KANTER

STORY: ALLAN WEISS

PRINCIPAL CAST: ELVIS PRESLEY (CHAD GATES), JOAN BLACKMAN (MAILE DUVAL) ANGELA LANSBURY (SARAH LEE GATES), NANCY WALTERS (ABIGAIL PRENTICE), ROLAND WINTERS (FRED GATES) AND JENNY MAXWELL (ELLIE CORBETT)

The freshly minted state of Hawaii (granted statehood in 1959) provided a gorgeous playground and enthusiastic welcome for the cast and crew of *Blue Hawaii*. In fact, Presley's fans in the Aloha State were so excited to see their idol in person that they followed him to various locations, creating security issues and disrupting filming with their screaming. Try as they might, *Blue Hawaii*'s sound engineers could not completely erase the fans' high-volume cheering from the soundtrack. In the film's opening scene at the Honolulu airport, Presley's fans can be heard distinctly in the background as he disembarks from the plane.

Reteaming with his *G.I. Blues* director Norman Taurog, Presley plays another soldier in *Blue Hawaii*, which casts him as Chad Gates, the heir to his family's pineapple business.

Returning home from his two-year stint in the army, Chad wants nothing more than to be with his sweetheart

Top: Presley makes a memorable entrance in *Blue Hawaii*. Bottom: Chad Gates (Presley) sings to his girlfriend, Maile (Joan Blackman), that he was "almost always true" to her.

Maile Duval (Joan Blackman), surf with his buddies and sing. Chad's aspirations don't jibe with the future his imperious but dotty mother, Sarah (Angela Lansbury), has already mapped out for her son; she insists that Chad drop his working-class girlfriend Maile and take his rightful place in society. So when Chad informs Sarah and his father, Fred (Roland Winters), that he wants to work as a tour guide, they naturally regard his career choice as beneath him.

Undaunted, Chad takes a position with a local tour company and soon finds himself escorting a beautiful school teacher, Abigail Prentice (Nancy Walters), and four teenage girls around the island. Before long, Chad realizes that he has his hands full with surly teenager Ellie Corbett (Jenny Maxell), a teacher who is starting to fall in love with him, and a girlfriend who's becoming more jealous by the day. Under the swaying palm trees, Chad cheerfully sorts out his romantic entanglements and his future role in the burgeoning state of Hawaii.

The first of three films Presley would make in Hawaii — the others being *Girls, Girls, Girls* (1962) and *Paradise, Hawaiian Style* (1966) — *Blue Hawaii* seemingly borrows a page from Presley's own life by making Chad Gates a returning soldier. Unlike his *Blue Hawaii* character, however, Presley often neglected to take charge of his own life and film career. He allowed his longtime manager Colonel Parker to choose his acting roles, even though Presley wasn't always happy with Parker's decisions.

Top: Maile models her new bikini for Chad. Bottom: Chad sings with his surfer/musician friends.

In *Blue Hawaii*, Presley seems to be enjoying himself. Although his character has some roguish moments, such as kissing a stewardess to make his girlfriend jealous, there's no malice to Chad, who shares a surprisingly mature relationship with Maile. Granted, she's concerned when Chad squires the beautiful schoolteacher, but Blackman invests Maile with a quiet strength and confidence that's tremendously appealing. She and Presley have an easy rapport that makes Chad and Maile a believable and likable screen couple.

Blackman, who would reunite with Presley on-screen in *Kid Galahad* (1962), fares better than Lansbury, who gives a broadly comedic performance in a one-dimensional role. Then entering the character actress phase of her career, where she often played mothers to actors less than 10 years her junior, Lansbury does what she can, but *Blue Hawaii* is not one of her shining moments in film. A year later, she would justly earn raves and an Academy Award nomination for her chilling performance as the ruthless mother of a brainwashed assassin in *The Manchurian Candidate* (1962).

Chad shows the sights to school teacher Abigail Prentice (Nancy Walters, to Presley's left) and her students (Christian Kay in front seat, Pamela Austin, Darlene Tompkins and Jenny Maxell, left to right in back seat). Opposite page: A surf lesson.

"Baby, I was almost always true to you. I was almost always true."

— sung by Chad Gates (Presley)

Of course, neither Lansbury nor anyone associated with *Blue Hawaii* probably expected critics to praise Presley's eighth film, which *Variety* called "a handsome, picture-postcard production crammed with typical South Seas musical hulaballo." Indeed, *Blue Hawaii* almost plays as more of a travelogue than a feature film, as Presley's character introduces his clients to such classic Hawaiian activities as luaus, hulas, and surfing. Though filmed mostly on Oahu, the final part of the film takes place on the island of Kauai at the Coco Palms Resort. The hotel reaped tremendous publicity from the film and enjoyed almost 40 successful years until it was destroyed by Hurricane Iniki in 1992.

A box office hit, *Blue Hawaii* was an even bigger smash as a record album. Featuring the hit single "Can't Help Falling in Love," the soundtrack album spent a total of 79 weeks on *Billboard*'s album chart, including 20 weeks in the number one spot.

SONGS IN BLUE HAWAII

"Blue Hawaii"

"Almost Always True"

"Aloha Oe"

"No More"

"Can't Help Falling in Love"

"Rock-a-Hula Baby"

"Moonlight Swim"

"Ku-u-i-po"

"Ito Eats"

"Slicin' Sand"

"Hawaiian Sunset"

"Beach Boy Blues"

"Island of Love"

"Hawaiian Wedding Song"

"Stepping Out of Line"

FOLLOW THAT DREAM (1962)

UNITED ARTISTS

DIRECTOR: GORDON DOUGLAS

SCREENPLAY: CHARLES LEDERER

BASED ON THE NOVEL "PIONEER, GO HOME!" BY RICHARD POWELL

PRINCIPAL CAST: ELVIS PRESLEY (TOBY KWIMPER), ARTHUR O'CONNELL (POP KWIMPER), ANNE HELM (HOLLY JONES), JOANNA MOORE (ALISHA CLAYPOOLE), SIMON OAKLAND (NICK) AND JACK KRUSCHEN (CARMINE)

P resley had played a naïve country boy in earlier films, but never one as completely clueless as Toby Kwimper, who "homesteads" on a Florida beach with his bumpkin family in *Follow That Dream*. If this broad comedy seems like an odd vehicle for Presley — especially in the wake of *Blue Hawaii* (1961) — *Follow That Dream* shrewdly tapped into the American public's taste for lowbrow, cornpone humor, which had propelled the CBS sitcom *The Beverly Hillbillies* to the top of the Nielsen ratings.

In fact, *Follow That Dream* pointedly evokes *The Beverly Hillbillies* in its depiction of a good-natured and tight-knit Southern clan running up against bankers and others who consider them rubes. Unlike the rags-to-riches millionaire Clampetts on the CBS sitcom, however, the Krimpers are dirt-poor; they subsist only on whatever they can squeeze out of the U.S. government: Toby's disability pay for a

Top: The Kwimpers, on the road to "homestead." Middle: Free beachfront property? Not if the superintendent of highways can help it. Bottom: A bait-and-tackle operation is born out of a cane pole, a diaper pin, and a banker who just happened to be driving by.

back injury he sustained while in the army, as well as the welfare Pa Kwimper (Arthur O'Connell) collects for each of the children he's adopted. The trouble is, one of those unofficially adopted orphans, Holly (Anne Helm), has more than a sister's feelings for Toby. She soon finds herself vying with state welfare bureaucrat Alisha Claypoole (Joanna Moore) for Toby's affections. He in turn keeps his distance from both women; if either of them get a little too close, he starts reciting multiplication tables until temptation passes.

Variety dubbed *Follow That Dream* "a kind of second cinematic cousin to *Tammy and the Bachelor* [a 1957 film starring Debbie Reynolds as a plucky Mississippi teenager]" in which "Presley portrays what amounts to a cross between Li'l Abner and male counterpart of Tammy." The entertainment trade paper conceded that "by Presley pix standards, it's above average"— a fair assessment of Gordon Douglas' film, which benefits greatly from the easygoing chemistry of Presley and O'Connell and a solid screenplay by Charles Lederer, whose credits included *His Girl Friday* (1940) and *Gentlemen Prefer Blondes* (1953).

Although *Follow That Dream*'s humor and tone may recall *No Time for Sergeants* (1958), Presley's ninth film is not nearly as simplistic as it initially appears. Based on Richard Powell's 1959 novel *Pioneer, Go Home!*, *Follow That Dream* is actually a good-natured satire of libertarianism.

Top: Holly (Anne Helm) listens as Pa (Arthur O'Connell) accompanies Toby (Presley) singing "Sound Advice." Middle: Toby's naiveté gets him mistaken for a bank robber instead of a good Samaritan looking for a loan. Bottom: Toby and Holly inform small-time crooks Carmine (Jack Kruschen) and Nick (Simon Oakland) there's no government authority on this beach.

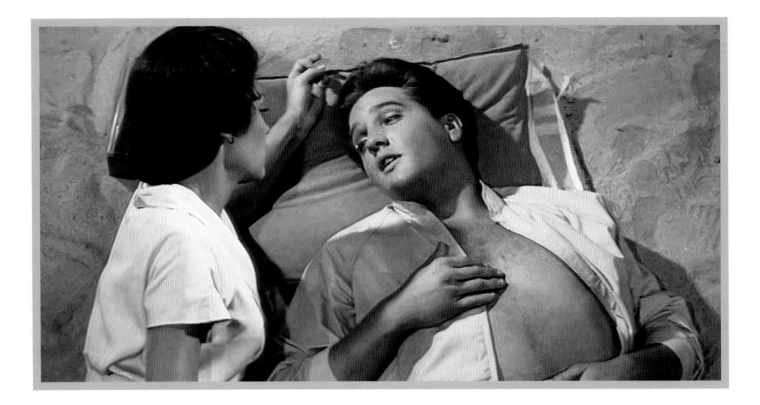

Toby charms Alisha Claypoole (Joanna Moore) with a song.

Pop Kwimper is suspicious of government and has taught Toby and the rest of his brood to be equally gun-shy around bureaucrats. The Kwimpers' distrust of government is established in the film's opening scenes, when they take a side road that's clearly marked closed and make themselves at home near the river. But when Mr. King (Alan Hewitt), the state supervisor of highways, drives the route to make sure it's pristine enough for the governor's planned ribbon-cutting ceremony and sees these "hillbillies" and their ramshackle shelter, he loses his temper. "Funny thing," Pop remarks, "I was just about to give him back his land. Then he turned nasty."

What first seems like paradise to Pop — a home 50 feet off the highway where, because of a legal oversight, neither state nor county has the authority to remove the Kwimpers — later turns into a countrified version of paradise lost. Once their story hits the papers and others realize there's land to be had if you homestead, a regular little community springs up. Unfortunately, that includes two small-time gangsters (Simon Oakland and Jack Kruschen), who run a floating craps game in a trailer. When they come on the scene, the target of the humor shifts, so that the bulk of the comedy derives from Toby's dealings with these petty crooks.

"Elvis hits the road to laughter and hits a new high in romance!"
— *Follow That Dream* tagline

Follow That Dream has the distinction of being the first Elvis movie to be filmed entirely on location — in Crystal River, Inverness, Ocala, and Yankeetown, Florida. There was a downside, though. Elvis recorded the soundtrack in July 1961 and drove to Crystal River a week later to begin filming. Summer in Florida can be brutal, and Elvis reportedly had to change his shirt 22 times in one day because he perspired so much. Shooting the gambling scenes was also problematic because it was illegal at the time, and they couldn't find a craps table to use for a prop. According to one of Elvis's "Memphis Mafia," the problem was solved when a couple of gamblers showed up and delivered the equipment on loan — no questions asked.

A box office disappointment that never ranked higher than fifth place on *Variety's* weekly box office chart, *Follow That Dream* was reportedly hated by Presley, who thought he looked fat in the film. Yet this amiable satirical comedy ultimately holds up better than many of Presley's other films, thanks to its change-of-pace storytelling, genial wit and appealing performances by the entire cast.

SONGS IN
FOLLOW THAT DREAM

"What a Wonderful Life"

"I'm Not the Marrying Kind"

"Sound Advice"

"Follow That Dream"

"Angel"

Top: Toby makes a point with the out-of-town "muscle" that Nick and Carmine hired. Middle: Toby tries to keep the welfare people from taking the twins away from his family. Bottom: Toby sings "Angel" to Holly.

KID GALAHAD (1962)

UNITED ARTISTS

DIRECTOR: PHIL KARLSON

SCREENPLAY: WILLIAM FAY

PRINCIPAL CAST: ELVIS PRESLEY (WALTER GULICK), GIG YOUNG (WILLY GROGAN), LOLA ALBRIGHT (DOLLY FLETCHER), JOAN BLACKMAN (ROSE GROGAN) AND CHARLES BRONSON (LEW NYACK)

"The man who can sing when he hasn't got a thing…he's a king" croons Elvis Presley as freewheeling, ex-G.I. Walter Gulick, riding on the back of a semi truck tailgate as it travels along the roadway. This attention-getting main title sequence, showcasing Presley's inimitable way with a catchy melody and crisp lyric, immediately sets the stage for his tenth feature film, the infectiously entertaining *Kid Galahad*.

A remake of the 1937 Warner Bros. boxing drama starring Edward G. Robinson and Humphrey Bogart, *Kid Galahad* was transformed into a star vehicle for Presley by television writer William Fay. While it lacks the grit and staccato energy of the original film directed by Michael Curtiz, Phil Karlson's *Kid Galahad* holds up surprisingly well, thanks to Karlson's no-nonsense direction, cinematographer Burnett Guffey's atmospheric visuals and the cast's uniformly fine performances.

Top: Walter Gulick (Presley) is straight out of the army and ready to start living. Bottom: Lola Albright as Dolly Fletcher. Albright rose to fame on television's *Peter Gunn*.

After the spirited opening number, army vet Walter Gulick arrives in New York's Catskills Moutains in search of a job. Wanting to set up an auto repair shop but short on cash, he takes a temporary position as sparring partner in a boxing training camp run by Willie Grogan (Gig Young) and his girlfriend, Dolly (Lola Albright). Although Willie regards the young man as little more than a rube with a talented right hook, he decides there's money to be made from Walter turning professional. Despite Dolly's misgivings, Willie christens Walter "Kid Galahad" after the most gallant and virtuous knight of King Arthur's Round Table.

Following a series of victories in the ring, Walter falls in love with Willie's sister, Rose (Joan Blackman), and decides to give up boxing for good. Unfortunately, Willie can't afford for Kid Galahad to hang up his gloves; he owes too much money to local gangster Otto Danzig (David Lewis), who coerces Willie into fixing the Kid's last fight against the experienced fighter Sugarboy Romero (real-life welterweight boxing champion Orlando de la Fuente).

Out of money and options, Willie begrudgingly agrees to Danzig's demands. Walter's trainer Lew (Charles Bronson), however, refuses to go along with the scheme and incurs the vicious wrath of Danzig's thugs. Arriving on the scene, Walter comes to the aid of his gravely injured trainer and sustains a severe beating. Exhausted and battered, Walter refuses to cancel the

Top: Rose Grogan (Joan Blackman) on the receiving end of an unwanted request. Bottom: "This sort of thing is legal?" Willy Grogan (Gig Young) and Dolly Fletcher watch Walter in the ring.

fight; he enters the ring, determined to face his formidable opponent — and win the love of Rose.

Though he looks rather doughy in *Kid Galahad* (he was reportedly overweight when filming began), Presley still makes a convincing boxer. He was also thrilled to train for the film with former world welterweight champion Mushy Callahan and his assistant Al Silvani, who had worked with boxing greats Floyd Patterson and Rocky Graziano.

Presley's sparring is undeniably impressive, but he shines brightest in *Kid Galahad*'s musical sequences. Granted, there are instances when he bursts into song that may strike contemporary viewers as bordering on ridiculous. Case in point: Walter sings "Riding the Rainbow" to Willie and Lew as they tool around in a truck (!). He fares better performing "King of the Whole Wide World" during the film's opening credits and serenading his *Blue Hawaii* co-star Blackman with the romantic ballad, "Home Is Where the Heart Is."

Walter sings "It wouldn't mean a thing if I could be a king." Opposite page top: Walter sings "I Got Lucky" to Rose. Bottom: Kid Galahad braces himself between rounds during the big fight.

"Don't push me, Willy. I'm a grease monkey that won't slide so easily!"

— Walter Gulick (Presley)

"Hey, Walter! In case you want to duck once in a while, it ain't against the rules!"

— Charles Bronson (Lew Nyack) to Presley (Walter Gulick) who is getting pummeled in a boxing match

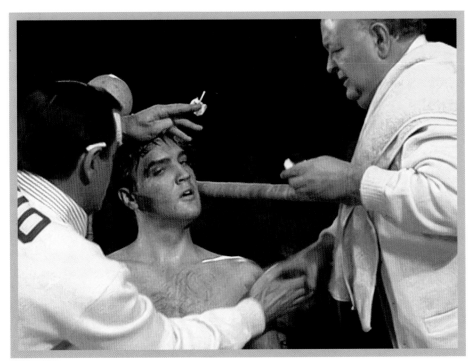

SONGS IN KID GALAHAD

"King of the Whole Wide World"

"This Is Living"

"Riding the Rainbow"

"Home Is Where the Heart Is"

"I Got Lucky"

"A Whistling Tune"

Kid Galahad also benefits considerably from the work of a top-notch supporting cast, headed by Young and Bronson, who reportedly clashed with Presley during the film's production. Other standouts in the cast include Lewis as the ruthless gangster Danzig and Albright, taking on a role played by Bette Davis in the original film.

A modest box office success, *Kid Galahad* received a begrudgingly positive review from the *New York Times'* Bosley Crowther, who called it "a moderately genial entertainment. It's not explosive, but it has the cheerful top of a lightly romantic contrivance that ranges between comedy and spoof."

"Presley packs the screen's biggest wallop…with the gals…with the gloves… with the guitar!"

— *Kid Galahad* tagline

Walter is instantly smitten upon meeting Rose Grogan.

GIRLS! GIRLS! GIRLS! (1962)

PARAMOUNT PICTURES

DIRECTOR: NORMAN TAUROG

SCREENPLAY: EDWARD ANHALT AND ALLAN WEISS

PRINCIPAL CAST: ELVIS PRESLEY (ROSS CARPENTER), STELLA STEVENS (ROBIN GATNER), JEREMY SLATE (WESLEY JOHNSON) AND LAUREL GOODWIN (LAUREL DODGE)

*G*irls! Girls! Girls! is the Rodney Dangerfield of Presley films: his follow-up to *Kid Galahad* (1962) gets no respect, even though it's far better than most of his big-screen vehicles. The only Presley film to receive a Golden Globe nomination for Best Motion Picture–Musical or Comedy, *Girls! Girls! Girls!* also boasts Academy Award–winning talent behind the camera. Director Norman Taurog had won the golden statuette for the Depression-era tearjerker *Skippy* (1931). And *Girls! Girls! Girls!* co-screenwriter Edward Anhalt had received the Academy Award for Best Motion Picture Story for *Panic in the Streets* (1950). Critics may have pronounced the film's songs "forgettable," but the *Girls! Girls! Girls!* soundtrack nonetheless earned a a gold record; the single "Return to Sender" stayed on the *Billboard* charts for 14 weeks, reaching number two for five of those weeks.

Since *Blue Hawaii* (1961) had been Presley's biggest box office hit to date, Paramount Pictures hoped to strike

Top: Ross Carpenter (Elvis) between sets at the Pirates Den. Bottom: Keeping it clean for the family audiences: Ross and Laurel (Laurel Goodwin) share a chaste kiss goodnight.

Top: Ross with his nemesis, Wesley Johnson (Jeremy Slate).
Bottom: Ross serenades Mama Stavros (Lili Valenty) as Laurel
(Laurel Goodwin, far left) watches.

gold a second time by also setting *Girls! Girls! Girls!* in the fledgling Aloha State. Early working titles for the film included *A Girl in Every Port* and *Welcome Aboard*, but the final title was taken from a song originally written for The Coasters, a 1950s-era rock and roll vocal group. Filming began on Kauai and around Honolulu in April of 1962, when 8,000 Presley fans mobbed their idol at the Honolulu Airport. In the crowd Presley lost a tie clasp and a favorite diamond ring; the latter was returned to him the next morning.

Accompanying Presley was his "Memphis Mafia," some of whom can be seen as extras in a tuna-fishing scene. A member of Presley's entourage, Alan Fortas, recalled that "Taurog was one of the few directors who'd ever tell Elvis what to do. Elvis loved it . . . and he bought Taurog a Cadillac to show his appreciation." The director in turn got Presley the piano he'd requested so he and his friends could relax between takes by singing gospel music — a far less risky diversion than practicing karate, which Presley had been studying since 1958. Worried that his star would injure himself, Taurog tried to curb Presley's habit of breaking upwards of 40 boards nightly with his bare hands (Presley had earned his black belt in 1960). Producer Hal B. Wallis finally stepped in and told Presley to stop practicing karate until the film completed production.

In *Girls! Girls! Girls!* Presley portrays Ross Carpenter, a young man raised by Mama and Papa Stavros (Lili Valenty and Frank Puglia) after his father died. Ross captains one of their sport-fishing boats and lives on the sailboat *West Wind*, which Ross built with his father. But when Mama's ailing health forces the couple to sell their little fleet, including the *West Wind* to Wesley Johnson (Jeremy Slate), a wealthy rake, Ross takes a second job singing at the Pirates Den nightclub, hoping to earn the money he needs to

buy back the *West Wind*. Meanwhile, Ross finds himself torn between sexy nightclub singer Robin Gantner (Stella Stevens) and "nice girl" heiress Laurel Dodge (Laurel Goodwin, whom Presley briefly dated during filming).

Ross and Laurel sail the *West Wind*. Although filmed on location, *Girls! Girls! Girls!* uses obvious process shots of the Pacific Ocean in many scenes.

The narrative formula that began to take shape in *G.I. Blues* (1960) and *Blue Hawaii* (1961) solidified in *Girls! Girls! Girls!*: musical numbers take precedence over character development and story; the latter adheres to the shopworn "boy meets girl(s)" scenario with numbing regularity. The assembly-line plots and breezy tone of these films wasn't lost on Presley, who had initially aspired to be taken seriously as an actor. He may have been "giving the people want they want," but playing the "bad boy" who's tender-hearted and polite beneath his rebel façade in lightweight musical comedies effectively reduced Presley to the level of a "one-trick pony" on-screen.

In *Girls! Girls! Girls!*, Presley's "bad boy" hero is devoted to his adoptive parents, especially Mama Stavros; he warbles a ballad for her on the couple's anniversary. Taurog's film also presents the rock and roll idol as a natural with children. While visiting the family of his ship's mate Chen (Guy Lee), Ross bonds with two neighborhood children, Mai Ling and Tai Ling (Ginny and Elizabeth Tiu). Regrettably, these scenes with Chen's family and friends traffic in racial stereotypes:

"You're Sir Galahad, Don Juan, and Cassanova rolled into one. If it isn't this boat, it's girls. Girls! Girls! Girls!"

— Robin Gantner (Stella Stevens)

"You must get a lot of this."

"Quite a bit. You'd think if nothing else the fish smell would keep them away."

— Fishing boat charter's flirtatious wife (Ann McCrea) to Ross Carpenter (Presley)

SONGS IN GIRLS! GIRLS! GIRLS!

"Girls! Girls! Girls!"

"I Don't Wanna Be Tied"

"Where Do You Come From"

"I Don't Want To"

"We'll Be Together"

"A Boy Like Me, A Girl Like You"

"Earth Boy"

"Return to Sender"

"Thanks to the Rolling Sea"

"Song of the Shrimp"

"The Walls Have Ears"

"We're Coming in Loaded"

"Because of Love"

Top: Ross performs an impromptu number with two neighborhood children. Bottom: Ross and Laurel dance a tango in her apartment.

Chen is called "Number one son," the Chinese characters are referred to as "inscrutable" and pidgin English is mocked. However, Presley has a nice rapport with the child actors and performs an amusing, Chinese-themed number with them.

The film's soundtrack album earned Presley another gold record and features a solid combination of ballads — "We'll Be Together" and "Because of Love" — and toe-tapping, up-tempo songs like "Return to Sender," "I Don't Wanna Be Tied" and the title track. There's even a fun novelty song, the tango-inspired "The Walls Have Ears," which Presley's character sings to the nice-girl heiress as they dance in her apartment.

Although *Girls! Girls! Girls!* only grossed a fifth of what *Blue Hawaii* took at the box office, the nation's motion picture exhibitors were impressed by Presley's consistent drawing power. At years' end, they voted him the fifth biggest box office attraction in Quigley Publication's annual "Top Ten Moneymakers Poll."

Presley sings one of his signature hits in *Girls! Girls! Girls!*: "Return to Sender."

"I'm just a red-blooded boy and I can't stop thinkin' about girls! Girls! Girls! Girls!"

— Presley (from the title song, by Jerry Leiber and Mike Stoller)

IT HAPPENED AT THE WORLD'S FAIR (1962)

MGM

DIRECTOR: NORMAN TAUROG

SCREENPLAY: SI ROSE AND SEAMAN JACOBS

PRINCIPAL CAST: ELVIS PRESLEY (MIKE EDWARDS), VICKY TIU (SUE-LIN), JOAN O'BRIEN (DIANE WARREN), GARY LOCKWOOD (DANNY BURKE), YVONNE CRAIG (DOROTHY) AND H.M. WYNANT (VINCE BRADLEY)

Ten million people passed through the turnstiles of Century 21, otherwise known as the Seattle World's Fair, between April 21 and October 21, 1962. The biggest thrill for many of them might have been taking in the view from the top of the brand-new Space Needle, or pondering the future in the World of Tomorrow exhibit. But for those lucky enough to attend it during 10 days in September, the fair provided a rare opportunity to watch rock and roll royalty at work, when Elvis Presley arrived to shoot scenes for *It Happened at the World's Fair*, an atypical comedy in which adventure and romance take a backseat to a rare demonstration of Presley's domestic side on-screen.

Reteaming with *Girls! Girls! Girls!* director Norman Taurog, Presley stars as pilot Mike Edwards, whose livelihood is jeopardized when his plane is impounded. Looking for work, Mike and best friend Danny Burke

Top: Buddies Danny Burke (Gary Lockwood) and Mike Edwards (Presley) earn some scratch at the controls of their crop duster. Middle: Playboy Mike works his seductive charm on his latest would-be conquest Dorothy Johnson (Yvonne Craig). Bottom: Little Sue-Lin (Vicky Tiu) shares a secret with her new best friend, Mike.

(Gary Lockwood) head to Seattle, where they meet farmer Walter Ling (Kam Tong) and his little niece Sue-Lin (Vicky Tiu). When Walter cannot take Sue-Lin to the World's Fair, Mike volunteers to chaperone her. A special day for Sue-Lin turns into an even better one for playboy Mike after he meets pretty nurse Diane Warren (Joan O'Brien). Unsure of what else to do when Uncle Walter fails to pick up Sue-Lin, Mike continues to take care of Sue-Lin. In the meantime, Danny accepts a cargo job from shady Seattle businessman Vince Bradley (H.M. Wynant), a development that further complicates Mike's life.

There are three competing elements in *It Happened at the World's Fair*: the love story between Mike and Diane; the crime drama that ensnares Mike, due to his friendship with Danny; and the family tale, in which Mike becomes a father figure to Sue-Lin. Admittedly, the narrative's disparate elements do not mesh together smoothly. The subplot depicting Danny's involvement with the shady businessman is particularly incongruous; then again, Mike's friendship with the degenerate gambler Danny smacks of contrivance. And while the romance complements the family story, it unfolds in routine fashion; there's a chaste, borderline dull quality to Presley's scenes with O'Brien. In contrast, he generates real chemistry with co-star Yvonne Craig, who plays a date Mike literally chases around the room.

Top: After a fun day at the world's fair, a tuckered-out Sue-Lin and Mike head home on the monorail. Middle: Kurt Russell makes his big-screen debut at 11 as the nameless kid who kicks Mike. He would go on to earn a 1979 Emmy nomination for playing the King in the made-for-television film *Elvis*. Bottom: Mike's injured leg is just the prescription to garner some tender loving care from nurse Diane Warren (Joan O'Brien, center).

The most satisfying element in *It Happened at the World's Fair* is the relationship between Mike and Sue-Lin, played by Tiu. Now known as Vicky Tiu Cayetano, Presley's co-star went on to found a commercial laundry company and serve as Hawaii Governor Ben Cayetano's first lady from 1994 to 2002. Only 6 when she made her one and only big-screen appearance, she replaced her sister Ginny in the role after a scheduling conflict arose when the older girl (who, along with siblings Elizabeth and Alexander, had earlier appeared with Presley in 1962's *Girls! Girls! Girls!*) was invited to play piano for President John F. Kennedy at the White House. The pint-sized actress and Presley are terrific together, as the lothario discovers his latent paternal instinct. At a time when he was still one of the world's most eligible bachelors, *It Happened at the World's Fair* offered a tantalizing glimpse of the domestic side of the performer famous for those suggestively swiveling hips.

Another child of note appears alongside Presley in the picture, as an 11-year-old Kurt Russell made his feature-film debut as a little boy who kicks Mike in the shin. Years later, Russell would go on to acting stardom, thanks to Presley. A working actor throughout his childhood, he spent time in the Disney stable where he made *The Computer Wore Tennis Shoes* (1969) and *Now You See Him, Now You Don't* (1972) and flirted with a career in baseball, doing time in the minor leagues. Two years after Presley's 1977 death, director John Carpenter cast Russell as the titular character in the acclaimed Presley made-for-television biopic *Elvis: The Movie* (1979). It would prove to be Russell's breakthrough role, earning him a Lead Actor Emmy

Appreciative bystanders look on as Mike serenades Diane with a romantic song. Opposite page: Mike and Diane celebrate the fair and their budding relationship by stepping out with the marching band.

"I guess you can call me one of the last pioneers, going where the wind blows, wherever I'm needed."

— Mike Edwards (Presley) talking about his job as a freelance pilot nomination and he would go on to star in such films as *Escape from New York* (1981), *Silkwood* (1983) and *Tombstone* (1993).

"When I worked with him, he [Presley] made a very strong impression on me, in terms of his work," Russell would later relate. "He was 27 years old, and, when I played him, I was 27. I had a lot of research available to me to be able to draw on, but, at the end of the day, it was really my memory of who he was, having worked with him for a couple of weeks. His demeanor and style was what I drew from."

It was Washington state's governor, Albert D. Rosellini, who suggested to MGM that the studio set one of Presley's films at the world's fair. Presley also received a $250,000 offer to perform at the fair, which his manager Colonel Tom Parker turned down. Perhaps it is no coincidence that *It Happened at the World's Fair* occasionally plays like a travelogue celebrating fair highlights that would outlast the fair itself, such as the Space Needle and the monorail.

When the film opened in the spring of 1963, neither that keepsake view of the fair nor Presley's charisma was enough to satisfy *Variety*. The trade publication complained that the movie's 10 songs destroyed the movie's tempo and declared in its review, "[*It Happened at the World's Fair* is] tedious going for all but the most confirmed of Presley's young admirers." The insult turned out to be prophetic, as the movie gained little traction at the box office, earning just $2.5 million, good enough only for the number 55 spot in *Variety*'s rankings for the year. Nearly 50 years after it was made, it remains a minor Presley film, memorable for its status as a souvenir of the long-vanished Century 21 World's Fair, and for the inspiration it gave Kurt Russell as he forged the role that would lead to an enduring career.

SONGS FROM IT HAPPENED AT THE WORLD'S FAIR

"I'm Falling in Love Tonight"

"Relax"

"How Would You Like to Be"

"Beyond the Bend"

"One Broken Heart for Sale"

"Cotton Candy Land"

"A World of Our Own"

"Take Me to the Fair"

"They Remind Me Too Much of You"

"Happy Ending"

FUN IN ACAPULCO (1963)

PARAMOUNT PICTURES

DIRECTOR: RICHARD THORPE

SCREENPLAY: ALLAN WEISS

PRINCIPAL CAST: ELVIS PRESLEY (MIKE WINDGREN), URSULA ANDRESS (MARGUERITA DAUPHIN), ELSA CARDENAS (DOLORES GOMEZ), PAUL LUKAS (MAXIMILLIAN), LARRY DOMASIN (RAOUL ALMEIDO) AND ALEJANDRO REY (MORENO)

While Presley was filming *Girls! Girls! Girls!* (1962) at Paramount Studios' Stage 5, producer Hal B. Wallis began to develop a story idea for his next film with the rock and roll idol. Inspired by a travel magazine story about Acapulco, Mexico's cliff divers, Wallis and writer Allan Weiss concocted a scenario in which Presley would play either a boat captain or an entertainer who befriends a native boy, who becomes the pint-sized equivalent of the star's real-life mentor/manager, Colonel Parker. And so the musical comedy/travelogue *Fun in Acapulco* became Presley's 13th film.

Reteaming with his *Jailhouse Rock* (1957) director Richard Thorpe, Presley stars as sailor Mike Windgren, who finds himself stranded in Acapulco without a work permit. With the help of Raoul Almeido (Larry Domasin), an enterprising shoeshine boy, Mike gets a temporary job as a lifeguard and fill-in singer at plush resort. Mike's charismatic good looks and affinity for Spanish rhythms

Top: Mike Windgren (Presley) works a short stint as a boat captain. Bottom: When his fortune changes, Mike Windgren sings "I Think I'm Gonna Like It Here."

make him easy sell for Raoul, who finds him additional singing gigs at Acapulco nightclubs.

As Mike's fame in Acapulco grows, he becomes involved with two beautiful women: Dolores Gomez (Elsa Cardenas), a celebrated female bullfighter, and Marguerita Dauphin (Ursula Andress), the daughter of the hotel's world-class chef Maximillian (Paul Lukas). Marguerita is also the boyfriend of Mike's co-worker and rival, Moreno (Alejandro Rey),

Mexico's greatest cliff diver, Moreno, who shows off regularly by diving from the 136-foot cliffs at La Quebrada, takes a dim view of Marguerita's attraction to Mike. Mike, however, is hiding a dark secret that he hopes to resolve in Acapulco, where circumstances and opportunistic people will ultimately force him to confront his past.

Initially, Presley's omnipresent manager Colonel Parker had been reluctant to allow his star travel to Mexico to film *Fun in Acapulco* (originally titled *Vacation in Acapulco*). In 1958, a false rumor had surfaced alleging that Presley had a misogynist view of Mexican women. Shrugging off that controversy, Presley had agreed to star in *Fun in Acapulco* for $200,000, as stipulated in his five-picture deal with Wallis. But Presley would never, in fact, actually go to Mexico to film any of *Fun in Acapulco*. All of his scenes would be shot in Hollywood with projected location backgrounds; a double would be used for long shots of his character on location.

Top: Larry Domasin gives a scene-stealing performance as shoeshine boy/business manager, Raoul Almeido.
Bottom: Mike's past as a trapeze star comes back to haunt him in Acapulco.

Production began on January 21, 1963, with a top-notch below-the-line team, including Academy Award–winning cinematographer Daniel Fapp and legendary costume designer Edith Head. *Fun in Acapulco* was Head's sixth Presley film. The eight-time Academy Award–winning costume designer had previously worked on *Loving You* (1957), *King Creole* (1958), *G.I. Blues* (1960), *Blue Hawaii* (1961) and *Girls! Girls! Girls!* (1962), and would later oversee costumes for *Roustabout* (1964), *Paradise Hawaiian Style* (1966) and *Easy Come, Easy Go* (1967). On *Fun in Acapulco*, Presley so admired Head's design of a navy blue and red cummerbund that he asked to keep it after filming wrapped.

On the second day of production, Presley went into the studio to record the film's 11, Latin-flavored songs in two marathon sessions. The songs' infectious rhythms bear the unmistakable influence of Herb Alpert & the Tijuana Brass, then riding high on the charts, and marked a stylistic departure for Presley, who performs them with great verve, especially "Guadalajara" and "Bossa Nova Baby", the latter hit number eight on *Billboard*'s Hot 100 chart. He also shows off some sensational moves in the film's musical sequences, including one number with a bullfighter's cape.

"The King's had official tasters. Why shouldn't I?" Mike (Elvis Presley) asks Marguerita Dauphin (Ursula Andress) and chef Maximillian (Paul Lukas).

"You sing pretty good for a gringo."

— Larry Domasin (Raoul Almeido) to Mike Windgren (Presley)

Fun in Acapulco's supporting cast is also notable. Best known to American audiences for her role in *Giant* (1956), Cardenas is excellent as the feisty matador who frequently speaks of herself in the third person ("Dolores likes you"). Andress, the first "Bond girl" in *Doctor No* (1962), lends *Fun in Acapulco* a touch of worldly sophistication, as does Lukas, the Hungarian-born character actor whose credits included Disney's *20,000 Leagues Under the Sea* (1954). All of them, even Presley, are nearly upstaged by Domasin, who effortlessly steals scenes as the pint-sized manager demanding a 50/50 split of Mike's earnings (an obvious jab at the excessive fees Colonel Parker infamously charged Presley). Domasin would later appear in the popular children's film *Island of the Blue Dolphins* (1964) and a handful of low-budget westerns.

When *Fun in Acapulco* opened nationwide on November 27, 1963, it appeared on *Variety*'s national box office charts for three weeks, peaking at number five. Among the Presley fans seeing *Fun in Acapulco* were the Beatles, who saw it at a Miami drive-in during the British rock and roll group's first American tour. According to a John Lennon interview in *The Beatles Anthology*, the "Fab Four" from Liverpool wouldn't actually meet Presley until August 27, 1965. As Lennon told it, Presley had no illusions about his film career:

"It's a pleasant, idyllic movie that never takes itself seriously and moves briskly under Richard Thorpe's direction."

— Howard Thompson, the *New York Times*

Moreno (Alejandro Rey) is not too pleased with Mike's interest in his girlfriend.

At first we couldn't make him out. I asked him if he was preparing new ideas for his next film and he drawled, "Ah sure am. Ah play a country boy with a guitar who meets a few gals along the way, and ah sing a few songs." We all looked at one another. Finally Presley and Colonel Parker laughed and explained that the only time they departed from that formula — for *Wild in the Country* — they lost money.

Happily, the Presley film formula works to entertaining effect in *Fun in Acapulco*. The show biz bible *Variety* was lukewarm about the overall film, but admitted that "Elvis Presley fans won't be disappointed." In contrast, the *New York Times'* Howard Thompson was surprisingly enthusiastic about *Fun in Acapulco*; he declared the "excellent color photography…positively eye-popping" and found the songs and the staging to be "bright and imaginative." As for Presley, Thompson wrote, "[he] has never seemed so relaxed and personable … This attractive travel poster for the famed Mexican resort is far and away his best musical feature to date."

Tensions mount as Mike finds himself torn between two beautiful women, Marguerita Dauphin and Dolores Gomez (Elsa Cardenas).

"Come With Elvis to Fabulous Acapulco!"

— *Fun in Acapulco* tagline

SONGS IN FUN IN ACAPULCO

"Fun in Acapulco"

"Vino, Dinero y Amor"

"Mexico"

"El Toro"

"Marguerita"

"The Bullfighter Was a Lady"

"No Room for Rhumba in a Sports Car"

"I Think I'm Gonna Like It Here"

"Bossa Nova Baby"

"You Can't Say No in Acapulco"

"Guadalajara"

Top: Presley in one of Edith Head's stylish costumes. Bottom: Mike faces a tough decision atop the cliffs in scenic Acapulco.

KISSIN' COUSINS (1964)

MGM

DIRECTOR: GENE NELSON

SCREENPLAY: GERALD DRAYSON ADAMS AND GENE NELSON

PRINCIPAL CAST: ELVIS PRESLEY (LIEUTENANT JOSH MORGAN/JODIE TATUM), ARTHUR O'CONNELL (PAPPY TATUM), GLENDA FARRELL (MA TATUM), JACK ALBERTSON (CAPTAIN ROBERT JASON SALBO), PAMELA AUSTIN (SELENA TATUM), CYNTHIA PEPPER (CORPORAL MIDGE RILEY) AND YVONNE CRAIG (AZALEA TATUM)

A low-budget quickie produced by schlock maven Sam Katzman, *Kissin' Cousins* is the antithesis of Presley's *Viva Las Vegas* (1964). Whereas that MGM film is a polished and comparatively lavish musical comedy that ranks among Presley's best films, this down-home piece of hillbilly kitsch is no more than serviceable, despite Presley's likable performance in his first dual role.

Infamous in Hollywood for cranking out 10 films a year with titles like *Mark of the Gorilla* (1950) and *Jungle Moon Men* (1955), Katzman reportedly found a penny-pinching ally in Colonel Parker, who had been dismayed when *Viva Las Vegas* went way over budget (shot before *Kissin' Cousins'*, *Viva Las Vegas* was released after it). To save money — and prevent *Kissin' Cousins* budget from cutting into his and Presley's share of the profits — Parker had the songs recorded in Nashville, with fewer musicians than usual, instead of Hollywood.

Katzman and Parker's tight fisted approach to *Kissin' Cousins* is readily evident in the cheap look of the film, set

Top: Back in uniform: Presley as the likable Lieutenant Josh Morgan. Bottom: Captain Salbo (Jack Albertson) informs serviceman Josh Morgan what his fate will be if their mission fails.

in Tennessee but shot on Southern California locations. The threadbare storyline casts Presley as army Lieutenant Josh Morgan, dispatched to Big Smokey Mountain to convince Pappy Tatum (Arthur O'Connell) to let the Pentagon build an ICM missile base on his property. Since Morgan's from the area and distantly related to the Tatum clan, his commanding officers believe he'll have better luck with Pappy, an ornery backwoods sort prone to shooting at military personnel coming on his land.

Accompanying Captain Salbo (Jack Albertson) and his military team to Tatum's mountain home, Josh discovers that he bears an uncanny resemblance to Pappy's son Jodie (Presley in an ill-fitting strawberry blonde wig). While Jodie takes an instant dislike to his cousin, Pappy's daughters Azalea (Yvonne Craig) and Selena (Pamela Austin) fawn over Josh. To complicate matters, 13 man-hungry beauties known as the Kittyhawks set their sights on Josh and his fellow soldiers. Unless Josh can win over Pappy Tatum in the short time allotted him, he runs the risk of permanent exile to a remote military outpost in Greenland.

Kissin' Cousins was directed by actor/dancer Gene Nelson, who had won the Golden Globe for Most Promising Newcomer for *Tea for Two* (1950) and co-starred in *Oklahoma!* (1955). After fracturing his pelvis in a 1957 accident, Nelson turned to directing film and television. As film historian Stuart Galbraith IV noted in his 2007 review of the *Kissin' Cousins* DVD, Nelson drew upon his dance training to stage the film's most elaborate production numbers, "Barefoot Ballad" and

Top: Captain Salbo and Josh en route to Pa Tatum's mountaintop home. Bottom: "There's Gold in the Mountains." Josh (Elvis Presley) with cousins Azalea and Selena.

Josh Morgan (left) meets lookalike cousin Jodie as cousins Selena (Pamela Austin) and Azalea (Yvonne Craig) look on.

"Once Is Enough," which evoke the energetic choreography of *Seven Brides for Seven Brothers* (1954). These two production numbers add a much-needed dose of pizzazz to a film that otherwise meanders to its foregone conclusion.

For Presley, the accelerated shooting schedule of *Kissin' Cousins* only reinforced his own misgivings about the film. As Nelson later told Peter Guralnick, author of *Careless Love: The Unmaking of Elvis Presley*, "He [Presley] came to me the last week and said he didn't like to work this way, it wasn't worth it. He said he knew what kind of pressure I was under, and he volunteered to get sick or show up late if it would help. I thanked him and said to hang in, it was *my* problem."

Presley also detested wearing a wig, which reminded him of his own blonde hair, before he began dying his hair black in homage to Roy Orbison. According to co-star Craig, "It was really traumatic for him. He didn't want to come out of the dressing room with the blond wig on. I figured other things were happening and I said to [director] Gene Nelson, 'What's the hang-up this morning?, And Gene said, 'Well, it's a problem. Elvis feels that he looks odd in the blond wig and really he doesn't have the guts to get up and get out here yet. But don't anybody make any remarks like "Gee, you sure look funny with the blond wig on.'"

SONGS IN KISSIN' COUSINS

"Kissin' Cousins"

"One Boy, Two Little Girls"

"There's Gold in the Mountains"

"Catchin' On Fast"

"Barefoot Ballad"

"Once Is Enough"

"Smoky Mountain Boy"

"Tender Feeling"

Of course, the wig was a minor annoyance compared to the injury co-star Glenda Farrell (as Ma Tatum) suffered during the making of *Kissin' Cousins*. While shooting a scene where Ma Tatum flips Jodie off a porch, Farrell broke her neck. As a result, she wore a neck brace for the duration of the production.

Presley himself narrowly escaped serious injury when the brakes gave out on the mobile home he was driving down California's Big Bear Mountain. He skillfully maneuvered past the precipitous drops on Highway 38 to bring the mobile home safely to a stop at the bottom of this winding mountain road.

Released to generally negative reviews in the spring of 1964 — the *New York Times'* Howard Thompson dismissed it as "tired, strained and familiar stuff" — *Kissin' Cousins* turned a tidy profit, grossing nearly $3 million (it cost approximately $800,000). And to the surprise of many critics, the Writers Guild of America nominated it for Best Written American Musical; that's quite an accomplishment for a film that even die-hard Presley fans regard as one of the weakest of his career.

"What are you doing with my face?"

— Jodie Tatum (Presley) to Josh Morgan (Presley)

Top: Ma Tatum (Glenda Farrell) describes the mountain meal of possum tails she has just served her guests as Josh listens. Bottom: The magic of split-screen: two Presleys for the price of one.

VIVA LAS VEGAS (1964)

MGM

DIRECTOR: GEORGE SIDNEY

SCREENPLAY: SALLY BENSON

PRINCIPAL CAST: ELVIS PRESLEY (LUCKY JACKSON), ANN-MARGRET (RUSTY MARTIN), CESARE DANOVA (COUNT ELMO MANCINI), WILLIAM DEMAREST (MR. MARTIN) AND NICKY BLAIR (SHORTY FARNSWORTH)

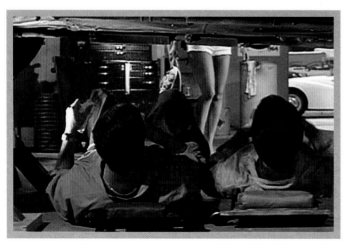

Quality was not a hallmark of Elvis Presley's 1960s-era musicals. The King of rock and roll once harbored the ambition of becoming a serious actor, but *Blue Hawaii*'s (1961) big box office gave manager Colonel Tom Parker all the ammunition he needed to convince the star that his cinematic future lay in romantic musical comedy. Presley's attitude toward this development might have been summed up by the name of one of his hit songs, "Baby, I Don't Care," as he put out one forgettable movie after the next like so many sausages. What makes *Viva Las Vegas* so startling is how it transcends the boilerplate formula of Presley's earlier romantic musical comedies, thanks to superior production values, a charismatic co-star, and a livelier, more engaged Presley.

Presley plays Lucky Jackson, a racecar driver who has come to Las Vegas to drive in the city's first-ever grand prix. When he meets Rusty (Ann-Margret), a flame-

Top: At the Flamingo to raise cash for his engine, racecar driver Lucky Jackson (Presley) wonders if a one-armed bandit can solve his problems. Bottom: Count Elmo Mancini (Cesare Donava, left) and Lucky get their first look at Rusty (Ann-Margret) from under a car.

haired swimming instructor, Lucky's ambitions widen as he dedicates himself to winning not just the race, but also the beauty's heart. Challenging Lucky for the white flag and the woman is friendly rival Count Elmo Mancini (Cesare Danova). Rusty herself is the biggest roadblock to Lucky's desire. They may sing beautiful music together, but her disapproval of racing works to keep them apart.

The first of Presley's films to cast him as a singing racecar driver — *Spinout* (1966) and *Speedway* (1968) are the others — *Viva Las Vegas* is thin and predictable at the story level. The pedestrian level of the writing is disappointing, given the pedigree of screenwriter Sally Benson, a novelist and *New Yorker* short story writer who had previously collaborated on the screenplay for Alfred Hitchcock's *Shadow of a Doubt* (1943). That Benson's heart was not completely in this latest assignment is most evident in the *Viva Las Vegas* scene in which Rusty describes the wonders of the Hoover Dam in what even she admits sounds like tour guide spiel.

Although Benson's script never rises above the hackneyed level of a "boy-meets-girl, boy-sings-to-girl" scenario, *Viva Las Vegas* is still supremely entertaining and easily one of Presley's best films. Budgeted at $1 million, it had the advantage of a relatively lengthy shooting schedule (two months as opposed to 17 days on Presley's *Kissin' Cousins*). In 24-year-old David Winters, the movie had a first-time feature choreographer with something to prove. And in George Sidney, an old MGM

Top: Rusty and Lucky check each other out while they check her motor. Bottom: Lucky strikes a pose at the Swingers Club before segueing into "The Yellow Rose of Texas."

Lucky strikes a familiar pose as he fronts the band.

hand whose credits included *Anchors Aweigh* (1945), *Annie Get Your Gun* (1950), and most recently the film that made Ann-Margret a star, *Bye Bye Birdie* (1963), *Viva Las Vegas* had a director who knew how to shoot a musical for maximum impact.

The ultimate key to the movie's success is Presley's co-star Ann-Margret. Then 22 years old, the dancer and singer's vivacious performances had already earned her the nickname "the female Elvis." Of all of his female co-stars, she is the one who matches him in talent and sheer star power. Certainly, Presley was as dazzled by her as were the fans. Despite the fact that he already had a steady girlfriend in teenager Priscilla Beaulieu — and that Ann-Margret was dating future producer Burt Sugarman — the pair's affair quickly became gossip column fodder. Some 30 years later, Ann-Margret told television host Charlie Rose, "Our relationship was very strong and very serious and very real. We went together for about a year." They remained lifelong friends.

"I don't work for anybody. I never run second to anybody, and one more thing, I intend to win."

— Lucky Jackson (Presley), declaring his Las Vegas Grand Prix intentions

"The electricity between them was instant and could have easily lit up the unplugged Vegas Strip," remembered Presley's close friend Sonny West. "It was a high-voltage love affair almost from the start,"

The actress adds a spark to *Viva Las Vegas* in her energetic dance numbers and in her chemistry with Presley. They were a cute couple, although behind the scenes neither Presley nor Colonel Parker was charmed by what they perceived as Sidney's bias toward her. "[Elvis] suspected that Sidney was infatuated with his co-star, which was a major understatement," recalled West. "When Elvis saw in the dailies that Ann was getting plenty of flattering close-ups, while he was relegated to window dressing, he was certain something was up."

Parker eventually went over Sidney's head to producer Jack Cummings, demanding changes that resulted in the cutting of two of three duets and more evenly distributed close-ups. Luckily, Parker lost another battle when Sidney succeeded in adding an unplanned production number, Presley's cover of Ray Charles' "What'd I Say," at the end of the shoot. Although the scene sent the movie

"When there was something to push him a little bit, he could still have fun, and in [*Viva Las Vegas*], Ann-Margret pushed him.

— Steve Pond, author, *Elvis in Hollywood*

Rusty and Lucky get closer on the dance floor.

over budget, angering the cost-conscious Parker, it showcases Presley and Ann-Margret's sizzling chemistry to maximum advantage. The sequence also features a cast of young dancers, including 20-year-old Teri Garr, a decade before she achieved stardom in Mel Brooks' *Young Frankenstein* (1974).

When Presley, billed as "the Atomic-Powered Singer," first played Las Vegas in 1956 at the New Frontier's Venus Room, the town reacted coolly to the 21-year-old up-and-coming rock and roll star; the *Las Vegas Sun* dismissed his music as "uncouth." Sin City proved luckier for Presley this time out; critics may not have wholeheartedly embraced *Viva Las Vegas* when it debuted in May 1964, but they conceded that it had its charms. While *Variety* complained, "The film is designed to dazzle the eye, assault the ear and ignore the brain," it also admitted, "The sizzling combination of Elvis Presley and Ann-Margret is enough to carry *Viva Las Vegas* over the top." Howard Thompson in the *New York Times* cheered, "The picture, as directed by George Sidney, tools along rosily," even as he dismissed it as "about as pleasant and unimportant as a banana split." The public did not share the critics'

A jealous Lucky playfully breaks in on Rusty and Elmo's date. Opposite page top: Lucky channels Ray Charles on "What'd I Say" and brings down the house. Bottom: "Viva Las Vegas!" Lucky's rendition of the title tune makes him a serious contender in the talent contest.

"Elvis is at the wheel but Ann-Margret drives him wild!"

— *Viva Las Vegas* tagline

reservations about Presley's 15th film; filmgoers embraced it worldwide, as *Viva Las Vegas* racked up nearly $9.5 million at the box office.

Though Presley had once been a Las Vegas loser, *Viva Las Vegas* put him in the chips. The king of rock and roll became a king of the Strip with the film that gave Sin City an enduring theme song, even as it froze in time its star at his sexiest, insouciant best.

The racers zip past Las Vegas casinos as the Grand Prix begins.

SONGS IN VIVA LAS VEGAS

"Viva Las Vegas"

"If You Think I Don't Need You"

"The Lady Loves Me"

"I Need Somebody to Lean On"

"C'mon Everybody"

"Tomorrow and Forever"

"Santa Lucia"

"What I'd Say"

"In my opinion, *Viva Las Vegas* was the best and most fun film experience of Elvis's movie career. He was in tremendous spirits because he was in love with someone who appeared to be his physical and spiritual equal."

— Presley friend Sonny West

Top: Ann-Margret as swimming instructor Rusty Martin. Her passionate, yearlong romance with Presley began during the filming of *Viva Las Vegas*. Bottom: Lucky fulfills a dream driving in the first annual Las Vegas Grand Prix.

ROUSTABOUT (1964)

PARAMOUNT PICTURES

DIRECTOR: JOHN RICH

SCREENPLAY: ANTHONY LAWRENCE AND ALLAN WEISS

PRINCIPAL CAST: ELVIS PRESLEY (CHARLIE ROGERS), BARBARA STANWYCK (MAGGIE MORGAN), JOAN FREEMAN (CATHY LEAN), LEIF ERICKSON (JOE LEAN), SUE ANE LANGDON (MADAME MIJANOU), PAT BUTTRAM (HARRY CARVER), JACK ALBERTSON (LOU) AND JOEL FLUELLEN (CODY)

In February of 1964, while the nation buzzed about a musical group from Liverpool on *The Ed Sullivan Show*, Elvis Presley and his friends enjoyed a different kind of pop entertainment. During a month long stay in Las Vegas, they took in shows by Fats Domino and Della Reese, watched a set by Don Rickles, and enjoyed the vocal stylings of crooner Tony Martin. When Presley's Vegas vacation came to an end, he bid farewell to Sin City and returned to Los Angeles to begin work on his 16th film, *Roustabout*.

Directed by John Rich, *Roustabout* casts Presley as Charlie Rogers, a motorcycle-riding rock and roller who winds up spending the night in jail after making quick work of angry frat boys in a parking lot brawl. Freed the next day, Charlie hits the road, where he has a near-fatal run-in with Joe Lean (Leif Erickson), a fast-driving carnival worker. While his bike is in the shop, Charlie accepts Joe's offer to work as a

Top: Charlie Rogers (Presley) enjoys the freedom of the open road. Bottom: Elvis Presley (with Joan Freeman and Barbara Stanwyck) was a seasoned movie star by the time he made *Roustabout*, his 16th film.

roustabout, i.e., an all-around carnival worker, for a few days.

At the carnival grounds, the businesswoman running the operation, Maggie Morgan (Barbara Stanwyck), immediately connects with Charlie because they're kindred spirits: unsentimental, honest and always aware of the bottom line. In contrast, Joe's pretty daughter Cathy (Joan Freeman) is initially standoffish to Charlie, but he soon wins her over with a serenade atop the Ferris wheel.

Charlie's musical talents begin drawing crowds, and before long he's promoted from roustabout to headline attraction at the "Girlie Show," where scantily clad dancers gyrate while he performs center stage. Offered a higher-paying gig elsewhere, Charlie faces a difficult decision: does he go for the money or stay with Cathy and the carnival workers, whom he considers family?

The casting of four-time Academy Award nominee Barbara Stanwyck enhanced *Roustabout*'s appeal for middle-aged and older filmgoers and gave this otherwise formulaic Presley vehicle a dose of old-fashioned star power. Though she did not know it yet, *Roustabout* would mark a turning point in Stanwyck's career. She made only one more feature film, the thriller *The Night Walker* (1964) before turning her attention to television, where she enjoyed great success as the star of the western drama, *The Big Valley*. In *Roustabout*, she shares the screen with her *Sorry, Wrong Number* (1948) co-star

Top: Cathy Lean (Joan Freeman) gives Charlie a tour of the carnival grounds. Bottom: Carnival attraction Madame Mijanou (Sue Ane Langdon) reads Charlie's fortune in a crystal ball.

Leif Erickson, who went on to star in the television series, *The High Chaparral.*

The talent at the helm of *Roustabout* came from the television world as well. John Rich had directed episodes of the westerns *Gunsmoke* and *Bonanza* and the first three seasons of *The Dick Van Dyke Show.* Although Rich claimed to know little about musicals and nothing about Presley, producer Hal B. Wallis hired him to direct *Roustabout.* It proved to be a demanding assignment for Rich, who tried to accommodate Presley, who wanted to perform his own fight scenes without a stunt double, *and* work around the star's entourage, who hung around the film's full-scale carnival set, which the studio had constructed on a cattle ranch outside Los Angeles.

On the cusp of 30 when *Roustabout* was shot, Presley keeps the gyrations to an absolute minimum in the film's musical numbers. His performing style is closer to that of musical statesmen like Dean Martin and Frank Sinatra than his rock and roll contemporaries. Even in the film's up-tempo numbers, Presley does little more than snap his fingers or clap his hands. Other songs he croons while strolling casually or sitting down.

Roustabout was released in November of 1964, three months after the Beatles' film *A Hard Day's Night,* and it suffered by comparison, both critically and commercially. But Presley's instincts about his image and material proved astute, as *Roustabout* went

SONGS IN ROUSTABOUT

"Roustabout"

"Poison Ivy League"

"Wheels on My Heels"

"It's a Wonderful World"

"It's Carnival Time"

"Carny Town"

"One Track Heart"

"Hard Knocks"

"Little Egypt"

"Big Love, Big Heartache"

"There's a Brand New Day on the Horizon"

on to become one of his highest grossing films; the soundtrack album went to number one on the *Billboard* charts, selling nearly half a million copies. And *Roustabout* screenwriters Anthony Lawrence and Allan Weiss received a Writers Guild of America nomination for Best Written American Musical; they lost to *Mary Poppins'* screenwriters Bill Walsh and Don DaGradi.

As 1964 drew to a close, Beatlemania was at fever pitch, and Presley, though generous in his public remarks about the British Invasion, was still finding his way in the new cultural landscape. He wanted to grow as a performer, but continued to cling to what had worked phenomenally well before. The shaggy mop-top was in, but Presley wore his hair in *Roustabout* as he had for over a decade: coiffed and oiled. But even as fashion changed around him, Presley had good reason to trust his taste. It had, after all, made him the biggest star in the world.

"I like white sheets and bright lights, and a lotta dough in my pocket."

— Charlie Rogers (Presley) to Cody (Joel Fluellen)

Opposite page: Charlie charms Cathy with a Ferris wheel serenade.
Top: Charlie whips up business with a rousing song on the midway.
Bottom: Charlie gives the crowd a sample of the spectacle they'll find inside the tent.

PART 3

1965-1969

ELVIS PRESLEY: 1965-1969

In August 1965, a quartet of British musicians dropped by Presley's California home for an informal jam session. The Beatles had been longtime fans, and they told Presley they had taken much of their musical inspiration from him — even though Presley hadn't performed live in four years, and the only Presley albums currently charting were his movie soundtracks and re-releases.

Then 30 years old, Presley was losing touch with the youth market he'd helped revolutionize just 10 years earlier. The swagger was still there, but Presley's rock and roll glory days seemed behind him, as he musically veered toward a "middle of the road" sound that attracted older audiences. It appeared that the "Fab Four" from Liverpool had deposed the King as rock and roll royalty.

Presley was also frustrated by the increasingly lackluster quality of his films. Watching him croon and chase girls in one formulaic musical comedy after another, it was hard to

PRESLEY'S LEADING LADIES, 1965-1969

INA BALIN
Charro! (1969)

In 1960, the Brooklyn-born beauty made the cover of *Life*; the following year, the Hollywood Foreign Press named Balin an "International Star of Tomorrow." Sadly, the hype never translated into lasting, above-the-title stardom for the actress, who received fine reviews for her performances in such films as *From the Terrace* (1960), *The Comancheros* (1961) and the cult film *The Projectionist* (1970).

DONNA DOUGLAS
Frankie and Johnny (1966)

Forever typecast as Ellie Mae Clampett, the critter-loving blonde bombshell of *The Beverly Hillbillies*, Douglas made only a handful of television appearances after the sitcom ended its run in 1971. Nor did she ever make another feature film after co-starring with Presley in *Frankie and Johnny*. Deeply religious, Douglas instead turned her focus to singing gospel music and doing charitable work.

SHELLEY FABARES
Girl Happy (1965), *Spinout* (1966) and *Clambake* (1967)

One of Presley's all-time favorite leading ladies, Fabares virtually grew up on camera. She made her television debut at age 10 and later became a household name playing Mary Stone on *The Donna Reed Show*. Aside from the Presley films, Fabares co-starred with British rockers Herman's Hermits in *Hold On!* (1966). She later found steady work in television, most notably on the sitcom *Coach*.

believe that Presley had once aspired to be another Marlon Brando. Critics who had praised his dramatic efforts in *Kid Galahad* (1958) and *Flaming Star* (1960) no longer even bothered to review many of his later films.

By all accounts, Presley was creatively stymied and clearly in need of a change. His frustrations began to manifest in erratic mood shifts. Quiet and humble one minute, he would become temperamental and hurl household objects across the room in the next. Presley worried about his looks. He obsessed over his weight and ate light meals of soup or peanut butter and banana sandwiches.

Throughout the late 1950s and early 1960s, he had surrounded himself with a group of old friends and colleagues who became known as the "Memphis Mafia." The Mafia had been Presley's one source of comfort and camaraderie. They partied and played together. Occasionally, they even worked together — in the recording studio or on the road. The Mafia loved their "boss," even when he threw things. Presley, however, was now spending more time with the girl who appeared to be "the One"— Priscilla — and the boys began to drift away, into other careers or relationships of their own. Priscilla had become Presley's own "Yoko Ono."

"Bachelorhood."

— Presley citing the reason he'd given up his own (bachelorhood)

MARY ANN MOBLEY
Harum Scarum (1965)

After being crowned Miss America in 1959, the Mississippi native embarked on a film and television career that earned her a Golden Globe for "Most Promising Newcomer–Female" in 1965. She appeared in such 1960s-era television series as *The Man from U.N.C.L.E.* and *Mission: Impossible* and co-starred in the Jerry Lewis comedy, *Three on a Couch* (1966).

MARY TYLER MOORE
Change of Habit (1969)

After *The Dick Van Dyke Show* went off the air in 1966, the television icon made the leap to the big screen, albeit with mixed results. She co-starred with Julie Andrews and Carol Channing in the musical *Thoroughly Modern Millie* (1967) and a pair of forgotten comedies, *What's So Bad About Feeling Good?* (1967) and *Don't Just Stand There!* (1968), before joining Presley in *Change of Habit*.

NANCY SINATRA
Speedway (1968)

Between 1964 and 1968, the pop star appeared in seven feature films, most of them low-budget entries like *The Ghost in the Invisible Bikini* (1966) and *The Wild Angels* (1966), starring Peter Fonda and Bruce Dern as Hell's Angels bikers. Sinatra enjoyed more success on the pop charts, where she scored number one hits with "These Boots Are Made for Walkin'" and "Somethin' Stupid," a duet

Nevertheless, Presley channeled his energies into his personal life and pet projects. He and his father, Vernon, contributed regularly to charitable causes. He spent more time remodeling Graceland, and in 1967, he bought a 163-acre Mississippi ranch he dubbed the Circle G, where he and Priscilla would spend their free time horseback riding. Also in 1967, he and Priscilla wed at the Aladdin Hotel in Las Vegas. The intimate ceremony was followed by a press conference at which photographers yelled for the couple to pose this way and that and to "smile big — look happy!" Elvis quipped, "How can you look happy when you're scared? I'm a little bit nervous, you know…Ed Sullivan didn't scare me this much."

As so happened, Presley had little to fear. The political turmoil of the late 1960s, along with the changes in his personal life, would open new doors for creative expression. He would earn his first Grammy Award for Best Sacred Performance for his gospel album, *How Great Thou Art.* In 1968, nine months to the day after he had wed Priscilla, their daughter, Lisa Marie, was born. He performed in public for the first time in eight years — an informal concert mixing songs and stories that was featured in his 1968 NBC special, *Elvis.* A mixture of production numbers and jam sessions with fellow musicians, *Elvis* was enthusiastically received by critics and fans alike as Presley's comeback. For the first time in years, he took the opportunity to pour his heart and soul into his music, most memorably in the autobiographical song "Guitar Man." He also commented musically on the deaths of Robert Kennedy and

Presley's singing has a magnetic effect on the Circle Z's guests in *Tickle Me* (1965).

Presley goes native in the musical finale of *Paradise Hawaiian Style* (1966).

Martin Luther King Jr. and silenced naysayers with his electrifying performances of such songs as the gospel-themed "If I Could Dream." As Jon Landau wrote in *Eye* magazine, "He sang with the kind of power people no longer expect of rock and roll singers. He moved his body with a lack of pretension and effort that must have made Jim Morrison green with envy."

The next year, Presley fulfilled — with perhaps a sigh of relief — his contractual obligation to Hollywood. As *Midnight Cowboy* (1969) entered preproduction, a studio executive sent director John Schlesinger a memo: "If we could clean this up and add a few songs, it could be a great vehicle for Elvis Presley." Indeed, Presley had been interested in the role of Joe Buck, which eventually went to Jon Voight. Instead, he would go on to do *Change of Habit* (1969) with Mary Tyler Moore. Though the film was critically panned, Presley was happy to wrap his film career and return to the recording studio and concert hall.

In July of 1969, Presley was booked for a four-week, 57-show engagement at the Las Vegas International Hotel. Although the response to his 1956 appearance had been lukewarm at best, Vegas was now ready for him. The engagement broke all previous attendance records and received rave reviews from both audiences and critics. At the age of 34, the King had regained his rock and roll throne.

"No, no, I won't. I'm going to do things now."

— Presley after recording his *Elvis* television special, responding to the idea that he might go make more "Elvis" movies

GIRL HAPPY (1965)

MGM

DIRECTOR: BORIS SAGAL

SCREENPLAY: HARVEY BULLOCK AND R.S. ALLEN

PRINCIPAL CAST: ELVIS PRESLEY (RUSTY WELLS), SHELLEY FABARES (VALERIE), GARY CROSBY (ANDY), MARY ANN MOBLEY (DEENA), FABRIZIO MIONI (ROMANO) AND HAROLD J. STONE (BIG FRANK)

Presley is in full command of his swiveling hips in *Girl Happy*, a likable musical comedy co-starring one of his all-time favorite leading ladies, Shelley Fabares. In Harvey Bullock and R.S. Allen's by-the-numbers screenplay, Presley portrays Rusty Wells, a singer hired by a thuggish Chicago club owner Big Frank (Harold J. Stone) to accompany his sheltered daughter Valerie (Fabares) to Fort Lauderdale for spring break. That's the perfunctory setup for *Girl Happy*, which confounds dire expectations with its jubilant energy, upbeat songs and ingratiating performances.

Girl Happy gets off to a lively start, as Rusty and Valerie duet on "Spring Break" en route to Fort Lauderdale in their snazzy convertibles. Arriving at the pastel-colored Seadrift Motel, they're greeted by the officious manager Penchill (John Fiedler), who lays down the soon-to-be-

Top: Rusty (Presley) and his bandmates hit the road for Fort Lauderdale. Middle: The Sea Drift Motel provides the colorful backdrop for much of the action in *Girl Happy*. Bottom: The Sea Drift Motel's persnickety manager (John Fiedler) informs the girls about the strict "no boys in the room" policy.

broken rule of "no boys in girls' rooms." Of course, the minute Rusty assumes Valerie will play nice, she attracts the attention of an Italian exchange student, Romano Alokta (Fabrizio Mioni). To keep Valerie away from the suave Romano while he simultaneously pursues the beautiful Deena (Mary Ann Mobley), Rusty resorts to increasingly outrageous tactics. Meanwhile, he begins to fall for Valerie himself, particularly after they share a dance in "Do the Clam," one of *Girl Happy*'s production numbers.

Girl Happy bounces through its 96 minutes like a beach ball in perpetual flight, thanks to Presley's charismatic screen presence. Appearing in virtually every scene, he carries himself with a worldly self-assurance that's striking, especially in the midst of the swimsuit-clad, all-American teenagers milling about in the background. Even Fabrizio Mioni's champagne-swilling Euro-sophisticate Romano pales in stark contrast to the star, who performs such fan favorites as "Puppet on a String" and "Do Not Disturb," along with "The Meanest Girl in Town": the latter is the one song not composed for the film and had previously been recorded by Bill Haley and the Comets in 1964, under the title "Yeah She's Evil."

Presley recorded *Girl Happy*'s 11 songs in June 1964 at Radio Recorders Studios in Hollywood. According to authors Roy Carr and Mick Farren in *Elvis: The Illustrated Record*, a slight inconsistency in the original mastering sped up Presley's voice on some of the songs, which

Top: Rusty's transfixed by the eye candy poolside.
Bottom: Rusty and his band perform the infectious "Wolf Call."

worked with the quick pace of the film. The official word on the mishap stated it was a way to bolster the title track and make it more upbeat. RCA released a new version of the title track in the 1990s for the compilation *Collectors Gold from the Movie Years*.

While Presley seems to be enjoying himself in *Girl Happy* (1965), he was growing increasingly disenchanted with the numbing familiarity of his films. According to Susan Doll's overview of Presley's film career for the website howstuffworks.com, he reportedly confided his feelings to *Girl Happy* director Sagal. Sagal in turn urged him to get off the Hollywood treadmill and go to New York to learn his craft.

"Every actor studies his trade," Sagal reportedly told Presley, "even those as good as Marlon Brando."

Unfortunately, Presley never did follow Sagal's advice. He continued making lightweight fare like *Girl Happy*, including two more with Fabares, *Spinout* (1966) and *Clambake* (1967). The only actress to play his love interest in three films, Fabares is an

Italian exchange student Romano Alotka (Fabrizio Mioni) introduces himself to Valerie (Shelley Fabares).

Top: Rusty puts the moves on a smitten Deena (Mary Ann Mobley). Bottom: Presley and dancers "Do the Clam."

Together at last: Rusty and Valerie.

SONGS IN GIRL HAPPY

"Girl Happy"

"Spring Fever"

"Fort Lauderdale Chamber of Commerce"

"Startin' Tonight"

"Wolf Call"

"Do Not Disturb"

"Cross My Heart and Hope to Die"

"She's the Meanest Girl in Town"

"Do the Clam"

"Puppet on a String"

"I've Got to Find My Baby"

appealing, girl-next-door type with a silky singing voice; she had previously topped the charts in 1962 with the single "Johnny Angel." One of Presley's favorite leading ladies, Fabares brings an infectious vitality to her role that nimbly complements Presley's confident star turn in *Girl Happy*.

"The steady stream of tunes…that's one thing — for those who care — you can always count on in a Presley frolic."

— Howard Thompson, the *New York Times*

TICKLE ME (1965)

ALLIED ARTISTS

DIRECTOR: NORMAN TAUROG

SCREENPLAY: ELWOOD ULLMAN AND EDWARD BERNDS

PRINCIPAL CAST: ELVIS PRESLEY (LONNIE BEALE/PANHANDLE KID), JOCELYN LANE (PAM MERRITT), JULIE ADAMS (VERA RADFORD), JACK MULLANEY (STANLEY POTTER), MERRY ANDERS (ESTELLE PENFIELD), EDWARD FAULKNER (BRAD BENTLEY) AND BILL WILLIAMS (DEPUTY SHERIFF JOHN STURDIVANT)

"Most moviegoers have long since forgotten the leering, heavy-lidded, gyrating young singer who was front-page news when he was first discovered a decade ago," entertainment journalist Peter Bart wrote from the set of *Tickle Me* in a Sunday *New York Times* feature that ran November 22, 1964. "But while no longer a national cause celebre, Elvis has managed to carve out a remarkable niche for himself in show business."

The article mixed subtle condescension for a youth culture the writer didn't respect or understand with skeptical admiration for Presley's astute manager, Colonel Tom Parker, an outsider who'd mastered Hollywood negotiations. "[Presley's] pictures usually have a tight shooting schedule so that he can make three or so a year," Bart wrote. "Elvis is paid between $600,000 and $1 million as straight salary for each picture plus a 50 percent share of the profits. Hence, in a good year he may earn as much as $5 million, a figure that makes him by far the highest paid movie star in Hollywood history."

Top: Lonnie Beale (Presley) sings of the "Long, Lonely Highway." Bottom: Exercise instructor Pam Meritt (Jocelyn Lane) gets her first gander at hunky cowboy Lonnie Beale.

Top: Presley in one of the film's Wild West fantasy sequences. Bottom: In the heat of the moment with co-star Adams, Presley winks at the audience.

Bart interviewed Colonel Parker, but apparently spoke with Presley for only a minute or two. He did obtain a particularly revealing quote from the star: "Ah want to be a better actor. Ah want to act in serious pictures. It will come someday. Ah don't want to rush it."

Bart's attempt to replicate Presley's Mississippi-Tennessee dialect smacks of elitism. The writer seemingly took Presley seriously as a commodity, but not as an artist; however, what is most striking about the article today is the fact that Presley revealed his true ambitions to a journalist he met only briefly.

Suffice to say, *Tickle Me* (1965) did not allow Presley to follow his aspirations. In his 18th feature film, he plays Lonnie Beals, an athletic rising star of the rodeo circuit who shows up in a dusty town for an off-season ranching job only to learn it's fallen through. Forced to earn a wage by singing in a local restaurant, Lonnie is spotted and snapped up by rancher Vera Radford (Julie Adams), whose Circle Z spread turns out to be a weight-loss spa for women. (In a concession to the sensitive sensibilities of male moviegoers, the only guests we actually see are slender beauties who've already benefited, apparently, from the expensive regimen.)

Vera would like Lonnie to pitch more than hay, but it's the exercise instructor, Pam Merritt (Jocelyn Lane), who catches his eye. There's a silly subplot, involving a stash of gold coins Pam's late grandfather hid in the nearby ghost town, which sets the stage for the film's farcical third act in a haunted house.

Directed in rote fashion by veteran Presley helmer Norman Taurog (*Blue Hawaii*), *Tickle Me* has the look, wit and narrative rhythm of a 1960s-era television show, peppered with a half-dozen fight scenes (the better to show off Presley's karate prowess). The star's relaxed performance compensates for the film's

glaring shortcomings, as does his chemistry with the British-born actress/model Lane, who bears an uncanny resemblance to Brigitte Bardot. She gives a spirited performance as Pam, who conceals her smoldering attraction to Lonnie by calling him a "sagebrush lothario" and a "prairie gigolo."

Tickle Me also benefits from a strong musical score, including "Dirty, Dirty Feeling," written by Jerry Leiber and Mike Stoller, and "Night Rider," by Doc Pomus and Mort Shuman. None of these songs was written specifically for the film. In fact, for the first time in his Hollywood career, Presley did not record and release a soundtrack album of fresh songs; instead, the *Tickle Me* soundtrack consists entirely of tracks he had recorded between 1960 and 1963 for earlier albums.

Recycling these songs was Colonel Parker's latest cost-cutting brainstorm. *Tickle Me* marked the first (and only) film he and Presley made with Allied Artists, which was then struggling to stay in business. Presley's $750,000 fee comprised a little more than half of the film's overall budget, so *Tickle Me* had to be shot on a

"Yes, it's Elvis as a singing, swinging cowboy, a rodeo-ridin', bronco-bustin' champ who's job is wrangling fillies on a dude ranch where the little girl with the big eyes is a cowboy's dream."

— Theatrical trailer

119

compressed schedule on the studio lot, with no allowance for location filming or lavish production numbers.

Soundtrack albums were a cornerstone of Colonel Parker's financial and marketing strategy, but he recognized that Allied Artists didn't have the money to commission and record an album of original songs. So he compiled tracks from Presley's well-received post-army sessions that had never been released as singles or received previous airplay to promote the film. It wasn't until 2005 that RCA assembled and released a CD soundtrack of *Tickle Me*.

Although it underwhelmed critics, the film did well enough at the box office to rescue Allied Artists from its dire financial straits. The Colonel knew very well what he was doing by refusing to book Presley on television, in nightclubs, or for any personal appearances; if Presley's fans wanted to see their idol, they had to buy a movie ticket — which they did, approximately three times a year in the 1960s.

"His movies produce profits with a consistency that continues to astonish Hollywood's money men and his records sell in the millions around the world," Bart wrote in his *New York Times* article. He went on to quote the confident and, for once, understated Colonel Parker: "We're doing all right the way we are going. Every year more money rolls in."

SONGS IN TICKLE ME

"Night Rider"

"I'm Yours"

"I Feel I've Known You Forever"

"Dirty, Dirty Feeling"

"Put the Blame on Me"

"Easy Question"

"Slowly But Surely"

"Long Lonely Highway"

"It Feels So Right"

Pam happily accepts Lonnie's promise that "slowly but surely, I'm gonna wear you down."

HARUM SCARUM (1965)

MGM

DIRECTOR: GENE NELSON

SCREENPLAY: GERALD DRAYSON ADAMS

PRINCIPAL CAST: ELVIS PRESLEY (JOHNNY TYRONNE), MARY ANN MOBLEY (PRINCESS SHALIMAR), FRAN JEFFRIES (AISHAH) AND MICHAEL ANSARA (PRINCE DRAGNA)

Desert sands by way of a Culver City soundstage, go-go dancing harem girls, and a turbaned Elvis Presley beckon in *Harum Scarum*, which netted the superstar his first $1 million salary for a film. Presley stars as Johnny Tyronne, a movie star in possession of a smooth baritone and a lethal karate chop. In the mythic Middle Eastern kingdom of Lunarkand to promote his latest picture, *Sands of the Desert,* Johnny meets up with the captivating Aishah (Fran Jeffries) and her escort, Prince Dragna (Michael Ansara).

"When you cross the mountains of the moon into our country, Mr. Tyronne, you'll be stepping back 2,000 years," Aishah tells him. "You'll find the pageantry and beauty almost unbelievable."

Soon thereafter, the unsuspecting lothario winds up kidnapped by a band of scoundrels who want him to assassinate their leader, King Toranshah (Philip Reed), with one of his mighty blows. Johnny escapes his captors

Top: Movie star Johnny Tyronne (Presley) in his latest film, *Sands of the Desert*. Bottom: It's kismet when Johnny meets Princess Shalimar (Mary Ann Mobley).

Top: Presley in one of *Harum Scarum*'s many fight scenes.
Bottom: Princess Shalimar in her royal lounge — one of the many elaborate sets created from leftover props and sets.

with the help of Zacha (Jay Novello), a comic rogue destined for sidekick duty as he ushers Johnny about the desert oasis. Along the way, Johnny meets and falls in love with the beautiful Princess Shalimar (Mary Ann Mobley), who is masquerading as a maid but is actually King Toranshah's daughter. In due course, Johnny saves the king's life and brings home a princess.

Shot in 18 days, *Harum Scarum* reunited Presley with his *Kissin' Cousins* (1964) director Gene Nelson and producer Sam Katzman, the low-budget impresario with a Midas touch at the box office. Katzman was infamous for never letting a little thing like a quality script get in the way of the bottom line, and *Harum Scarum* was no exception. Indeed, the narrative concocted by Gerald Drayson Adams was such a slapdash hack job that even Presley's penny-pinching manager Colonel Parker was angered by it. He reportedly fired off a letter to MGM brass, declaring that only "a 55th cousin to P.T. Barnum … [could] sell this picture."

Presley was equally frustrated by the rank cheesiness of *Harum Scarum*. According to Priscilla Presley, he knew all too well that "the plot was a joke, his character a fool, and the songs were disastrous." Despite his unhappiness, he soldiered on through the quickie production, which at least gave him the opportunity to work with some fine actors, most notably Michael Ansara, who had won acclaim playing the Native American chief Cochise in the 1950s television series *Broken Arrow*. In addition to Ansara, veteran stage and film actor Philip Reed brings a much-needed dose of class to *Harum Scarum* in his final screen role as King Toranshah. As for Presley's *Girl Happy* (1965) co-star Mary Ann Mobley, she does what she can with a largely decorative role.

Given the film's shoestring budget, *Harum Scarum* looks like a far more expensively mounted

Johnny's reflection serenades Princess Shalimar from her boudoir pool.

production, thanks to the ingenuity of art directors McClure Capps and George W. Davis and set decorators Henry Grace and Don Greenwood Jr. The quartet worked their magic by recycling leftover props and sets from older films, such as Cecil B. DeMille's biblical epic, *King of Kings* (1927). *Harum Scarum* also recycled the costumes from the 1944 and 1955 film versions of *Kismet*; Presley's costumes were personally designed by *Harum Scarum* director Nelson, who based them on Rudolph Valentino's outfits for *The Sheik* (1921). Priscilla Presley recalled in her memoirs that Presley loved wearing the loose-fitting arabesque outfits so much that he'd wear them home after a day on the set.

Presley may have loathed *Harum Scarum*, but in retrospect, his character's discovery of the ancient land of Lunarkand, crafted from leftover Hollywood biblical dramas, is a befitting metaphor for Presley's own spiritual journey during filming. Behind the scenes, he was seeking spiritual enlightenment and had immersed himself in eastern philosophy at Pasadena's Self-Realization Fellowship run by Sri Daya Mata, a disciple of Paramahansa Yogananda. According to his close friend and hair stylist, Larry Gellar, Presley was on a spiritual quest:

"You gotta be kidding. On second thought, you wouldn't wear your hair like that just for laughs!"

— Johnny Tyronne (Presley)

123

It was like a lightning bolt went right through him. He said, "Larry, I know the truth now. I don't believe in God anymore. Now I know that God is a living reality. He's everywhere. He's within us. He's in everyone's heart…. In fact, Larry, I want you to find me a monastery. I'm not making a move until you tell me what to do."

Presley's spiritual leanings apparently alarmed Colonel Parker, who tightened his already ironclad grip on his superstar client. Presley swallowed his bile and bowed to his Svengali-esque mentor's will, but churning out films like *Harum Scarum* was taking its toll on Presley's box office appeal. Although Quigley Publications ranked him seventh on its list of top-10 box office draws in 1965, the grosses for his films were dwindling. *Harum Scarum* came in 40th in *Variety*'s year-end survey of 1965's top-grossing films.

"Elvis brings the big beat to Baghdad in a riotous rockin' rollin' adventure spoof!"

— *Harum Scarum* tagline

Johnny unveils his new Middle Eastern–themed act in Las Vegas.

124

SONGS IN HARUM SCARUM

"Harem Holiday"

"My Desert Serenade"

"Go East — Young Man"

"Mirage"

"Kismet"

"Shake the Tambourine"

"Hey Little Girl"

"Golden Coins"

"So Close, Yet So Far (from Paradise)"

Top: "The scales do not balance, Mr. Tyronne." The sinister Aishah (Fran Jeffries, left) warns Johnny that escape is futile. Bottom: Michael Ansara as the villainous Prince Dragna.

FRANKIE AND JOHNNY (1966)

UNITED ARTISTS

DIRECTOR: FREDERICK DE CORDOVA

SCREENPLAY: ALEX GOTTLIEB

STORY: NAT PERRIN

PRINCIPAL CAST: ELVIS PRESLEY (JOHNNY), DONNA DOUGLAS (FRANKIE), HARRY MORGAN (CULLY), SUE ANE LANGDON (MITZI), NANCY KOVACK (NELLIE BLY), AUDREY CHRISTIE (PEG), ROBERT STRAUSS (BLACKIE) AND ANTHONY EISLEY (CLINT BRADEN)

Based on a turn-of-the-century ballad about a doomed love triangle between a torch singer and a gambler and his mistress, the period musical comedy *Frankie and Johnny* marked a departure for Presley, who had been starring in contemporary-themed fare like *Viva Las Vegas* (1964) and *Girl Happy* (1965). In this 1890s-era narrative set primarily aboard a Mississippi riverboat, Presley turns in a surprisingly low-key yet breezy performance as an inveterate gambler whose money woes are only compounded by his romantic misfortunes.

One of several films inspired by the 1904 song written by Hughie Cannon, *Frankie and Johnny* casts Presley as Johnny to Donna Douglas' Frankie. Employed by manager Clint Braden (Anthony Eisley), the couple performs a musical variety act that's far more harmonious than their off-stage relationship. Although she loves him deeply, Frankie refuses to marry Johnny until he promises to stop gambling away all his money.

Top: A glimpse of things to come, as provided in the film's opening frames. Bottom: "Love and trust: it's what makes a marriage great." Johnny (Presley) with Cully (Harry Morgan) and his domineering wife, Peg (Audrey Christie).

Top: Nellie Bly (Nancy Kovack) may just be the lucky redhead Johnny needs to change his fortune. Bottom: The potential consequences of Johnny's two-timing get a rehearsal onstage in the film's centerpiece musical number, "Frankie and Johnny."

Faced with her ultimatum, Johnny drags his sidekick Cully (Harry Morgan) with him to visit a gypsy, who tells Johnny that a redhead will enter his life to become his good-luck charm. Lo and behold, Braden's ex-love, Nellie Bly (Nancy Kovack), strolls aboard ship and into Johnny's affections.

Meanwhile, Cully has penned a new musical number entitled "Frankie and Johnny" that a visiting music producer thinks will be a smash hit in New York. Hoping to "earn" enough money to buy tickets for Frankie and himself to New York, Johnny enlists Nellie's help at the gambling tables. But while he sees greenbacks with this redhead, Frankie just sees red. Little does Frankie realize, however, that Nellie has eyes only for Braden, who is too busy warning Johnny away from Nellie to notice. When the hapless quartet of lovers lands in New Orleans for Mardi Gras, Frankie and Nellie conspire to masquerade as one another in order to teach Johnny a lesson in true love and luck.

Frankie and Johnny is one of Presley's least popular films, even among his hardcore fans. Writing for the website TCM.com, Jeff Stafford states, "If you really want to know what killed Elvis, it wasn't the drugs or the overeating; it was movies like *Frankie and Johnny*." While showcasing Presley's brand of "blue-eyed soul" and displaying a kind of tongue-in-cheek whimsy, the musical numbers are "non-hit wonders." According to Alanna Nash's 2003 book *The Colonel: The Extraordinary Story of Colonel Tom Parker and Elvis Presley*, *Frankie and Johnny*'s dismal box office results prompted Charles Boasberg, president of Paramount Film Distributing Corp., to fire off a letter to producer Hal B. Wallis: "*Frankie and Johnny* ... is dying all over the country, and this is his [Presley's] second poor picture in a row. If it weren't for you lifting him up with some good production in your pictures, Presley would be really dead by now."

Cully and Johnny test their luck with another redhead at the roulette table.

Today, however, some viewers take a slightly kinder view of *Frankie and Johnny,* rating it as more or less "average" on sites such as IMDb.com and forgiving the film for its many anachronisms; Presley wears his hair in his signature ducktail and comes across as contemporary, particularly when belting out songs in his bluesy, soulful style. Not that anyone was expecting strict verisimilitude from a Presley vehicle directed by De Cordova, whose credits included *Bedtime for Bonzo* (1952) and a string of television sitcoms (De Cordova would go on to direct and produce *The Tonight Show Starring Johnny Carson*). It's a gaudy Technicolor concoction that doesn't ask the viewer to take it too seriously, is occasionally witty and features fine comic turns by supporting cast members Morgan and Sue Anne Langdon (as the riverboat singer Mitzi).

As Frankie, Donna Douglas does a serviceable job in a role that failed to bring *The Beverly Hillbillies* star more feature film work. Like Presley, she was a member

"I'll lose my confidence if I pass up a hunch bet."

— Johnny (Presley)

SONGS IN FRANKIE AND JOHNNY

"Frankie and Johnny"

"Come Along"

"Petunia, the Gardener's Daughter"

"Chesay"

"What Every Woman Lives For"

"Look Out, Broadway"

"Beginner's Luck"

"Down by the Riverside"

"When the Saints Go Marching In"

"Shout It Out"

"Hard Luck"

"Please Don't Stop Loving Me"

"Everybody Come Aboard"

Top: Presley performs "Shout It Out." Bottom: Presley pays homage to his blues roots with the number "Hard Luck."

of the Self-Realization Fellowship, a worldwide spiritual organization based in Los Angeles promoting world peace and harmony. The two supposedly engaged in intellectual discussions, compared books, and meditated together — hardly the offscreen romance one might expect between Presley and a leading lady.

Presley recorded the song "Frankie and Johnny" in 1965, but he certainly wasn't the first to sing Cannon's classic ballad, originally titled "He Done Me Wrong." Several other singers and performers have interpreted "Frankie and Johnny," including Mae West, who performs it in *She Done Him Wrong* (1933). Presley's simple and unadorned version of the song is one of the film's musical highlights, along with a sequence pairing the star with an African-American boy, who accompanies him on a harmonica for a hard-luck blues number.

While *Frankie and Johnny* may not equal the popularity of Presley's other films, it remains enjoyable escapist fare. Encompassing everything from riverboat life to gypsy fortune-telling to Mardi Gras to good old-fashioned barroom fisticuffs, the film gives audiences rich visual entertainment and a playful musical romp that doesn't overstay its welcome.

Top:Johnny croons "Beginner's Luck" to Frankie in this fantasy sequence. Bottom: Presley offers a fresh take on "When the Saints Go Marching In."

PARADISE HAWAIIAN STYLE (1966)

PARAMOUNT PICTURES

DIRECTOR: MICHAEL D. MOORE

SCREENPLAY: ANTHONY LAWRENCE AND ALLAN WEISS

PRINCIPAL CAST: ELVIS PRESLEY (RICK RICHARDS), SUZANNA LEIGH (JUDY "FRIDAY" HUDSON), JAMES SHIGETA (DANNY KOHANA), DONNA BUTTERWORTH (JAN KOHANA), MARIANNA HILL (LANI KAIMANA), IRENE TSU (PUA), LINDA WONG (LEHUA KAWENA) AND JULIE PARRISH (JOANNA)

In 1966, the United States sent B-52s to bomb North Vietnam for the first time and antiwar protests raged across the country: but in the nation's movie theaters it was business as usual, with only one of the year's 10 highest-grossing films dealing with war. The year's top-grossing film was George Roy Hill's sweeping adaptation of James Michener's bestseller *Hawaii*, while Elvis Presley's third and final film set in the Aloha State, *Paradise Hawaiian Style* limped into 40th place on the year-end box office chart. It was directed by Michael D. Moore, who had previously served as assistant director on six Presley films. Taking the director's chair for the first time, Moore sadly failed to capture the charm of Presley's earlier Hawaiian-set films, *Blue Hawaii* (1961) and *Girls! Girls! Girls!* (1962).

Paradise Hawaiian Style features Presley as Rick Richards, a pilot with a past. Rick's flying record is spotless, but his womanizing gets him fired from every major airline. Needing a job, he turns up at the small

Top: Rick Richards (Presley) entertains Jan Kahana (Donna Butterworth, center) and her friends. Bottom: It's a dog's life for Presley, who serenades his four-legged co-stars in the film's campiest scene.

Top: Rick and Jan duet on "Datin'." Bottom: Three's company: Rick takes Jan on his date with Lani (Marianna Hill).

aircraft business of his friend, Danny Kohana (James Shigeta), and persuades him to take out a loan so they can go into business together: flying tourists in helicopters to pristine, out-of-the-way places.

Hardly reformed, Rick sweet-talks four ex-girlfriends working at resort hotels so they'll send business his way. The first stop is the Maui Sheraton in Lahaina, where Rick's former flame Lehua (Linda Wong) works. Next comes a visit to Hanalei Plantation Resort, where another ex-girlfriend, Lani (Marianna Hill) is a nightclub singer. Naturally, she invites Rick to get aboard the little cable car that descends into the nightclub, where she performs a husky-voiced song-and-dance number, "Scratch My Back (Then I'll Scratch Yours)," which turns into a duet with Rick. Then it's off to the Polynesian Cultural Center, where Rick joins old girlfriend Pua (Irene Tsu) in a duet of "Drums of the Islands."

Directed in perfunctory fashion by Moore, these scenes epitomize the threadbare quality of the film's narrative. There's barely a whiff of energy to Presley's scenes with his screen girlfriends in *Paradise Hawaiian Style* — until his high-flying lothario pays a visit to the Kahala Hilton Hotel, where Rick agrees to help *another* ex-girlfriend Joanna (Julie Parrish) transport a pack of show dogs to a rich woman on another island. What follows is one of the most embarrassing scenes in Presley's film career, when Rick lifts the ears of the dogs and sings "A Dog's Life" into them (it's a wonder he didn't get bitten).

There's also a fifth woman, Judy "Friday" Hudson (Suzanna Leigh), a wannabe pilot whom Danny hires as a secretary, then asks her to pretend to be married so that Rick will leave her alone. Naturally, Rick falls hard for "Friday," but Presley doesn't generate much in the way of chemistry with Leigh. In fact, he seems most energized and alive in *Paradise Hawaiian Style* when he's sharing the screen with the dogs, rather than

Rick, Jan and "Friday" (Suzanna Leigh) prepare to help Jan's injured father, Danny (James Shigeta).

his two-legged co-stars — except for child actress Donna Butterworth, who plays Danny Kohana's daughter Jan.

Already a seasoned show business professional at 10 years old, Butterworth had sung on *The Andy Williams Show* and received a Golden Globe nomination for Most Promising Newcomer–Female for the Jerry Lewis comedy *The Family Jewels* (1965). Precocious but never obnoxious, she sings a couple of duets with Presley and performs a Polynesian-style version of "Won't You Come Home, Bill Bailey."

Interviewed years later by Joe Krein of the Official Elvis Presley Fan Club, Butterworth had only fond memories of working with Presley, who left her starstruck and tongue-tied on first meeting:

> I had to run up in his arms and say "Uncle Rick, Uncle Rick!" and explain what happened…. You know I had just met him a half hour before kind of shyly but when they said action and I had to run up into his arms and look straight into his beautiful face I just went blank, and I couldn't say my words and everybody started laughing. The director said cut! … I just froze. I was just thrilled to be looking at him.

"All ELVIS breaks loose in the Swinging, Swaying, Luau-ing South Seas!"

— *Paradise Hawaiian Style* tagline

Rick's womanizing ways catch up with him.

Butterworth soon recovered her composure and bonded with Presley, who delighted in playing pranks on the set and "had such an infectious laugh." By her account, Hawaii apparently agreed with Presley, who "was always in a really great mood" during the filming of *Paradise Hawaiian Style*.

At the time, Presley's good humor may have stemmed in part from his growing interest in spirituality and self-help. Through his friendship with hairstylist Larry Geller, Presley had begun spending time with Sri Daya Mata, the leader of the Self-Realization Fellowship, and poring over metaphysical and philosophical texts. When Presley finished shooting *Paradise Hawaiian Style*, he gave every crew member a copy of Joseph Benner's *The Impersonal Life*, which he found especially enlightening.

Released in June of 1966, *Paradise Hawaiian Style* inspired a collective yawn among film critics inured to the formulaic nature of Presley's films. As *Variety* reported, "Light script by Allan Weiss and Anthony Lawrence, based on former's original, serves more as a showcase for Presley's wares than as plottage but suffices to sock over the Presley lure."

Despite its stunning aerial photography and Presley's warm rapport with Butterworth, *Paradise Hawaiian Style* ranks as the weakest of the star's three films set in the Aloha State.

SONGS IN PARADISE HAWAIIAN STYLE

"Paradise Hawaiian Style"

"House of Sand"

"Queenie Wahine's Papaya"

"You Scratch My Back"

"Drums of the Islands"

"It's a Dog's Life"

"Datin'"

"Stop Where You Are"

"This Is My Heaven"

SPINOUT (1966)

MGM

DIRECTOR: NORMAN TAUROG

SCREENPLAY: THEODORE J. FLICKER AND GEORGE KIRGO

PRINCIPAL CAST: ELVIS PRESLEY (MIKE MCCOY), SHELLEY FABARES (CYNTHIA FOXHUGH), DIANE MCBAIN (DIANA ST. CLAIR), DEBORAH WALLEY (LES) AND CARL BETZ (HOWARD FOXHUGH)

In *Spinout*, Presley's sixth film with director Norman Taurog, the star portrays Mike McCoy, a drag strip racer forever ducking the advances of three smitten women. Pursued by scheming rich girl Cynthia Foxhugh (Shelley Fabares), Mike is offered $5,000 by her father, race-car magnate Howard Foxhugh (Carl Betz), to sing solo at her birthday. When Mike refuses the offer, Foxhugh sweetens the deal with a chance to drive his latest prototype race car. Unimpressed, Mike walks away, forcing Foxhugh to resort to blackmail.

Mike next catches the eye of Diana St. Clair (Diane McBain), a glamorous author of sex manuals for single women, who sizes him up as the perfect candidate for her latest project, *The Perfect American Male*. Further complicating matters is Les (Deborah Walley), the tomboy drummer in Mike's band. She too has a thing for him and joins Cynthia and Diana in the fight for Mike's affections.

Top: It's love at first sight for Cynthia Foxhugh (Shelley Fabares), when she sees rocker Mike McCoy (Presley) in his sleek Cobra 427. Middle: Diane McBain as Diana St. Clair, a character clearly modeled on *Sex and the Single Girl* author Helen Gurley Brown. Bottom: Mike offers Les (Deborah Walley) some practical tips for their impending stardom.

Deciding to teach the Foxhughs a lesson, Mike and his pals settle into the mansion next door and proceed to turn it into a rock and roll haven, where guests can indulge in the Frug, the Watusi and all those other wacky period dance crazes. Throughout the festivities, Mike remains front and center, a guitar-strumming pied piper, luring Foxhugh to his psychedelic den for a resolution that sets up the finale's sensational multicar drag race.

Directed with brisk efficiency by Taurog, *Spinout* is a standard-issue Presley film that's chiefly memorable for its score, featuring "Adam and Evil," "All That I Am," and the hyperenergetic "Smorgasboard." Although screenwriters Theodore J. Flicker and George Kirgo throw in a mild twist at the narrative's conclusion, they otherwise adhere to the basic cinematic template that almost all Presley films had followed since *Blue Hawaii* (1961): light-hearted musical comedy with plenty of songs and pretty girls ogling the star, held together by the most shopworn of plots.

In *Spinout*, however, the women don't just go wild over Presley's singing drag strip racer; they toss aside their boyfriends and husbands and latch onto him as if Mike's their last best hope for love. He in turn takes their frenzied adulation in stride and remains firmly committed to his bachelorhood. Leaping onto his prized Cobra, Mike declares "I'm not marrying you! I'm not marrying her! I'm not marrying anybody! I'm staying single! Single! Single! Single!"

Top: Presley performs the rollicking number "Beach Shack." Bottom: With three girls desperate to marry him, Mike hits the road in his Cobra 427.

For the film's racing sequences, Presley reported to Dodger Stadium; its parking lots were "used for the start and finish line of the racing scenes," according to Bob Smith, who was then overseeing stadium security. Interviewed by Brent Shyer for the Elvis Australia – Official Elvis Presley Fan Club website, Smith recalled how news of the star's presence at Dodger Stadium

Mike bears down on Foxhugh, (Carl Betz, right) and his assistant Phillip (Warren Berlinger).

was kept under wraps: "I remember that I saw Elvis, but he had bodyguards around him. They really didn't want it known that he was even out there."

Shyer also interviewed *Spinout* leading lady Shelley Fabares, who told him how much she loved shooting at Dodger Stadium, except for the day Taurog asked her to drive "a very hot red sports car" — and she didn't know how to drive a stick shift:

> He [Taurog] said, "Okay, get in the car and start back from over there and come in really fast and then swerve into that space there." And he said, "I'll have two people jump out of the way in front of you." "I looked at him and said, "Yeah right." And he said, "Yeah, what do you mean?" Anyway, I was terrified. I think the only person who was more terrified than I was, was the man who owned this car! He was sitting in it with me to help me at the beginning. I just kept saying to him, "I am so sorry, I promise you."

Spinout was the second of Fabares' three films with Presley; they would reteam the following year for *Clambake* (1967). Although Harry Medved includes *Spinout* in his 1978 book *The Fifty Worst Films of All Time (And How They Got That Way)*, Presley's 22nd film doesn't deserve to be lumped in with such disasters as *Robot Monster* (1953) and *Santa Claus Conquers the Martians* (1964). Yes, it's formulaic, but *Spinout* has a handful of genuinely witty scenes, as film critic/historian Stuart

"As soon as I domesticate you, get you housebroken, you'll be the best husband a girl ever had."

— Diana St. Clair (Diane McBain) to McCoy (Presley)

Galbraith IV noted in his review for the website dvdtalk.com: "Their [Flicker and Kargo's] script has fast, funny dialogue and eccentric characters who move the story in unexpected directions, faintly evoking classic screwball comedies like *The Palm Beach Story* (1942)." Granted, it's a *huge* stretch to draw a favorable comparison between *Spinout* and Preston Sturges' brilliant marital farce, but Flicker and Kirgo's script is far more clever and engaging than the usual, run-of-the-mill efforts churned out by hack writers for Presley films.

When MGM released *Spinout* in November of 1966, theater owners sponsored "The Perfect American Male Essay Contest"; winners received Presley records. The star's latest film did enough business to earn him the 10th-place slot on Quigley Publications' annual list of the top-10 moneymaking stars — the last time Presley made the list during his film career.

Ambitious and wealthy Howard Foxhugh plots with his equally conniving daughter Cynthia and his assistant Philip to get Mike to sing at her birthday. Betz also played Fabares' father on *The Donna Reed Show*.

"He drives a Duesenberg, he races a Cobra and he told me to go to hell."

— Howard Foxhugh (Carl Betz) about McCoy (Presley)

SONGS IN SPINOUT

"Spinout"

"I'll Be Back"

"All That I Am"

"Am I Ready"

"Stop, Look, Listen"

"Beach Shack"

"Adam and Evil"

"Smorgasboard"

Top: "Mr. Foxhugh, I think we have something in common — can we talk?" Sparks fly between Diana and Foxhugh. Bottom: A bachelor to the end.

Easy Come, Easy Go (1967)

Paramount Pictures

Director: John Rich

Screenplay: Allan Weiss and Anthony Lawrence

Principal Cast: Elvis Presley (Lieutenant Ted Jackson), Dodie Marshall (Jo Symington), Pat Priest (Dina Bishop), Pat Harrington Jr. (Judd Whitman), Skip Ward (Gil Carey), Frank McHugh (Captain Jack) and Elsa Lanchester (Madame Neherina)

For his eighth and last film with veteran producer Hal B. Wallis, Elvis Presley took on the role of a singing scuba diver (!) in *Easy Come, Easy Go*, a better-than-it-sounds musical comedy. Reteaming with the director and writers of *Roustabout* (1964), Presley ended his association with Wallis and Paramount Pictures on a relatively high note.

Presley stars as soon-to-be-discharged navy frogman Ted Jackson, an underwater demolitions expert. During a dive to deactivate an underwater mine, he finds a treasure chest in a sunken ship off the California coast. After his discharge from the navy, Ted tracks down the descendant of the ship's captain, Jo Symington (Dodie Marshall), at a yoga class taught by aging bohemian Madame Neherina (Elsa Lanchester).

A go-go dancing hippie, Jo agrees to help Ted and his beatnik buddy Judd (Pat Harrington Jr.) salvage the treasure from the wreck, using scuba equipment rented

Top: When no guitar is available, an oar will do for navy frogman Ted Jackson (Presley). Bottom: A spinning wheel display of pretty girls is enough to get Elvis Presley singing "The Love Machine" in *Easy Come, Easy Go*.

from Captain Jack (Frank McHugh). Potentially dire complications ensue when their salvage operation attracts the unwanted attention of Dina Bishop (Pat Priest) and her unscrupulous boyfriend Gil (Skip Ward), who will stop at nothing to get the treasure.

Although Presley reportedly clashed with director Rich during the filming of *Easy Come, Easy Go*, there's no trace of their tense relationship in Presley's amiable performance. The star also receives fine support from a cast comprised of Hollywood newcomers and veterans. Pat Priest of television's *The Munsters* effectively portrays the treacherous Dina, while Pat Harrington Jr. is interesting if underutilized as Ted's sidekick Judd. Providing comic relief is character actor Frank McHugh as the eccentric Captain Jack; the former vaudevillian retired from the screen after *Easy Come, Easy Go*, one of the 150-plus films McHugh made in a career dating back to the 1930s.

Of all the actors in *Easy Come, Easy Go*, however, no one makes a more vivid impression than Elsa Lanchester, who effortlessly steals scenes in her loopy turn as Madame Neherina. Best known for her iconic turn as *The Bride of Frankenstein* (1935), the two-time Academy Award nominee is a hoot in *Easy Come, Easy Go*, especially when she sings a memorable duet with Presley, "Yoga Is as Yoga Does."

Presley also establishes a nice rapport with Marshall, the British-born, Philadelphia-raised actress who'd made her film debut the year before in *Spinout*

Top: Ted and his navy buddies check out some beautiful women on a nearby boat. Bottom: The eccentric Captain Jack (Frank McHugh) on the hunt for treasure.

(1966). She more than holds her own opposite the star in *Easy Come, Easy Go* and seemed headed for stardom (or at least steady acting work). The reviewer for the entertainment trade paper *Variety* had pronounced Marshall "an excellent young actress with appealing warmth and looks for meatier sympathetic roles." Interviewed after the release of *Easy Come, Easy Go*, Marshall declared, "I want to be a star and I see no reason to conceal it. I want to get to the top of my profession … and I have the desire and some of the qualifications and I hope I can acquire the others."

Yet despite *Variety*'s glowing endorsement, the talented starlet inexplicably vanished from the show business radar. Aside from a few guest starring roles on late 1960s-era television series, Marshall never worked in Hollywood again.

The critical response to *Easy Come, Easy Go* was decidedly mixed. *Chicago Sun-Times* film critic Roger Ebert dutifully went to his first Presley film because he had to review it. "There is such a thing as a good movie musical," he wrote, "and then, I suppose, there must be such a thing as Presley movies like this one … produced with a minimum of care and with the sole purpose of contriving a plot, any plot, to fill in between when Elvis sings."

"There's something I should have told you before." Ted with Jo (Dodie Marshall).

Songs in Easy Come, Easy Go

"Easy Come, Easy Go"

"The Love Machine"

"Yoga Is as Yoga Does"

"You Gotta Stop"

"Sing, You Children"

"I'll Take Love"

Ebert called attention to Presley's "absolutely characterless features.... Here is one guy the wax museums will have no trouble getting right." As if that weren't vitriolic enough, the *Chicago Sun-Times* critic delivered this withering assessment of Presley: "After two dozen movies, [Presley] should have learned to talk by now. But it's still the same old slur we heard so many years ago on *The Ed Sullivan Show.*"

The Hollywood trade paper *Variety*, on the other hand, extolled *Easy Come, Easy Go* as "another well-made Hal B. Wallis production" with a "good balance of script and songs" and a "competent well-directed cast." As for Presley, *Variety's* reviewer thought the star looked "great and ageless" and predicted that "a generation from now, Elvis pix will be film festival items, just as the Busby Berkeley, Astaire-Rogers and Mae West pix are now."

Time has of course proved the *Variety* reviewer wrong; most of Presley's films are now regarded as lackluster star vehicles, indifferently cobbled together and rushed into theaters to make a fast buck — or so Colonel Parker hoped. By the time *Easy Come, Easy Go* hit theaters in March of 1967, Presley's box office popularity was beginning to wane. The film grossed a scant $1.92 million. It seemed even the King's most ardent fans were tiring of the Presley film formula.

> "Another well made Hal B. Wallis production...good balance of script and songs...competent, well-directed cast...diverting entertainment...Elvis looks great and ageless."
>
> — *Variety*

Dina (Pat Priest) works her wiles on Ted.

DOUBLE TROUBLE (1967)

MGM

DIRECTOR: NORMAN TAUROG

SCREENPLAY: MARK BRANDEL AND JO HEIMS

BASED ON THE NOVEL BY MARK BRANDEL

PRINCIPAL CAST: ELVIS PRESLEY (GUY LAMBERT), ANNETTE DAY (JILL CONWAY), JOHN WILLIAMS (GERALD WAVERLY), YVONNE ROMAIN (CLAIR DUNHAM) AND THE WIERE BROS (AS THEMSELVES)

In 1967, as the Mod movement permeated all facets of pop culture and Beatlemania spanned the globe, London reigned as the epicenter of "cool" in terms of music, fashion and film. The satirical flourishes and bravura, cutting-edge style of British films like *A Hard Day's Night* (1964) and *The Knack … And How to Get It* (1965) made Hollywood studio films of the era look positively old-hat. The frenetic energy and tongue-in-cheek humor of these films clearly influenced Presley's *Double Trouble* (1967), a genre-blurring pastiche of 007-style intrigue set against the backdrop of neon-lit discotheques in European locales.

Originally titled *You're Killing Me*, *Double Trouble* stars Presley as Guy Lambert, a rock star touring Europe with his band Georgie and the G-Men. While performing in London, Guy begins pursuing the prim and virginal

Top: Guy Lambert (Presley) sings the title track with his band, Georgie and the G-men. Middle: After being discovered by producer Judd Bernard in her parents' London shop, acting novice Annette Day was cast as Jill Conway in *Double Trouble*. Bottom: At a trendy discotheque, Guy Lambert is joined by his two competing female admirers, dark-haired seductress, Claire Dunham (Yvonne Romain) and Jill Conway.

Jill Conway (Annette Day), whom he first spies in the audience during a gig at a trendy discotheque. Guy also has an eye on the slinky Claire Dunham (Yvonne Romain), who's scheming to seduce Guy away from Jill.

Summoned by Jill's beloved uncle, the erudite Gerald Waverly (John Williams), Guy soon discovers that his latest squeeze is not only a very wealthy heiress but also an underage schoolgirl on the verge of turning 18. Disappointed, he mutters, "Seventeen will get me 20," as he promptly dispatches Jill and sets sail with his band mates to Brussels. Unbeknownst to him, Jill follows onboard and a series of deadly incidents force Guy to serve as her reluctant savior. A secondary storyline involving suitcases, one bearing diamonds, further convolutes the already disorienting shipboard hijinks, with two trench-coated jewel thieves (Chips Rafferty and Norman Rossington) in tow.

As red herrings pile up, *Double Trouble* veers into Agatha Christie territory by way of Lewis Carroll — a trippy, irreverent whodunit that lapses into brief spurts of chaos. Upon arrival in Belgium, Guy Lambert's fall through the rabbit hole is akin to crash landing in a Flemish Wonderland where no one is what he or she appear to be. Bizarre encounters with the Belgian denizens are often jarring as they greet Guy with toy guns and leers, leaving him to wander about the picturesque sets, perpetually stupefied. One particular

Top: Being a lady's man has its drawbacks as Guy discovers after getting punched out by a jealous rival. Middle: Snobbish Uncle Gerald (John Williams) shares some shocking news with Guy about Jill. Bottom: "You must like to travel to come all this way for a one-night stand." Guy (Presley) teases Claire after he discovering her in a smoky jazz club.

diversion turns unexpectedly harrowing after a hallucinatory carnival sequence, when a band of men in menacing masks corner the defenseless Jill on a dark street. Garishly lit, they taunt the horrified girl and, in an uncomfortable shift, the film's slapstick tone turns lethal. Warding off her would-be assailants, Jill soon finds herself alone with Morley (a sinister Michael Murphy), her Uncle's henchman. To her surprise, Jill learns that the assassin pursuing her and Guy was sent by trusted Uncle Gerald. "It's all been leading up to this," Morley informs her as he slips on a pair of black leather gloves, casually concluding, "There's an element of greed in all of us. The taste of your money has increased your uncle's appetite."

Arriving in the proverbial nick of time, Guy saves Jill and fends off Morley as the violence escalates into a well-choreographed fight scene that ends with Morley at the bottom of an empty pit. Offsetting the tension are the Wiere Brothers, playing a trio of mad detectives on the trail of the trouble-prone couple.

The convoluted plot manages to include some terrific musical interludes, specifically the erotically charged, "City by Night," which Presley sings in a smoky, cavernous jazz bar accompanied by a bluesy trombone. Also noteworthy are the boisterous title track and Presley's rousing rendition of the popular nursery rhyme, "Old MacDonald," which he performs on the back of a farm truck packed with clucking chickens, proving that the superstar was adept at turning *any* tune golden.

Portraying the conflicted Guy Lambert allowed Presley to stretch as an actor in improvised bits that reveal an unguarded vulnerability. In a scene where he steps out of a taxi into the oncoming headlights

Top: Guy launches into a rollicking rendition of "Old MacDonald had a Farm" for Jill. Bottom: "Will you give the trio a five-minute break? They are boring holes in the back of my neck!" Presley with the Wiere Brothers.

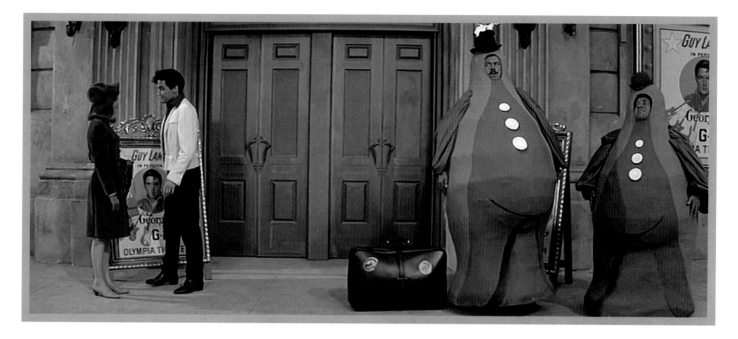

The two jewel thieves (Chips Rafferty and Norman Rossington) in disguise sidle up to Guy Lambert's suitcase.

of a speeding car Guy gasps, "Why don't you watch where you're going, you crazy idiot?!" He then swiftly ducks back inside the taxi, hurls himself across the back seat and exits on the opposite end, visibly shaken. Guy's relationship with the underage Jill is also riddled with anxiety and oddly reminiscent of Presley's own chaste, real-life romance with 14-year-old Priscilla Beaulieu. In her autobiography, *Elvis and Me*, Priscilla Presley states that Elvis refrained from having sexual relations with her until they were married — an interesting addendum to Guy Lambert's courtship of Jill Conway in *Double Trouble*.

Double Trouble was the only film made by Annette Day, whom producer Judd Bernard discovered working behind the counter of her parent's London antique shop. Finding her youth and beauty ideal for the part of Jill, Bernard not only hired the screen novice, he also had several of her slangy expressions written into the script. A sweet, likable presence, Day acquits herself nicely in the role and has an easy rapport with Presley that lends credibility to their storybook romance and the film's "happily married" ending — a bold departure for a Presley film. In most of his films, the star is aggressively pursued by several female admirers, yet remains unattached by film's end, as if an unspoken stipulation required Presley to stay single and available for the legions of girls who desired him. But in his 24th film, Presley's rockstar hero ties the knot at the conclusion of *Double Trouble*, which opened on April 5, 1967: less than a month before Presley wed fiancée Priscilla Beaulieu at Las Vegas' Aladdin Hotel on May 1.

SONGS IN DOUBLE TROUBLE

"Double Trouble"

"Baby, If You Give Me All Your Love"

"Could I Fall in Love"

"Long-Legged Girls with Short Dresses On"

"City of Night"

"Old MacDonald"

"I Love Only One Girl"

"There's So Much World to See"

"It Won't Be Long"

CLAMBAKE (1967)

UNITED ARTISTS

DIRECTOR: ARTHUR H. NADEL

SCREENPLAY: ARTHUR BROWNE, JR.

PRINCIPAL CAST: ELVIS PRESLEY (SCOTT HEYWARD), SHELLEY FABARES (DIANNE CARTER), WILL HUTCHINS (TOM WILSON), BILL BIXBY (JAMES J. JAMISON III), JAMES GREGORY (DUSTER HEYWARD) AND GARY MERRILL (SAM BURTON)

While *Clambake* may not be one of Presley's strongest films, it remains a favorite of many fans, including late-night television talk-show host Conan O'Brien. But according to Presley's road manager, the King hated the script, which was just another by-the-numbers musical comedy held together by the flimsiest of story lines. In fact, as Priscilla Presley later wrote in her memoir, the throwaway quality of his mid-1960s-era films so depressed Presley that he gained 30 pounds before shooting *Clambake*. The studio ordered him to lose weight before reporting to the set — as if he needed to add diet pills to his already growing dependency on drugs. Maybe Presley's subconscious mind was at work when, on the first day he was scheduled to begin shooting, he slipped in his bathroom and hit his head, causing a two-week delay for a film that he didn't want to make.

Nevertheless, the title song and its near mono-lyric ("Clam-bake, gonna have a clambake!") is undeniably

Top: Scott Heyward (Presley) and Tom Wilson (Will Hutchins), pauper, decide to switch identities. Middle: "You're the new skiing instructor?" Scott meets Dianne Carter (Shelley Fabares). Bottom: Scott attempts to win Dianne's heart with a song.

catchy, and Presley and co-star Shelley Fabares really click in their third and final film together, which puts a fun spin on Mark Twain's classic tale of *The Prince and the Pauper*.

Set in Florida but filmed primarily in Southern California, *Clambake* stars Presley as Scott Heyward, the son of wealthy oilman Duster Heyward (an appropriately larger-than-life James Gregory). When Scott meets impoverished water skiing instructor Tom Wilson (Will Hutchins) en route to Miami Beach, he decides to swap identities with Tom to see if the women swooning over him are after him or his father's money. Tom, meanwhile, is delighted to play the prince for a time, trading his motorcycle for an exotic sports convertible and a name, charge card, and checkbook that open doors to the best rooms, the finest food and drink, and more girls than he could ever imagine.

What's appealing about *Clambake* is that instead of two women vying for Presley's attention, the star has to compete for the woman he loves — and doesn't ply his trademark "bad boy" swagger to win her hand. So when Scott meets pretty gold digger Dianne Carter (Fabares) in his guise as the dirt-poor water skiing instructor, he never attempts to sweep her off her feet by revealing his true identity. He instead comes across as a decent, hard-working guy who can't buy her love. As a result, Dianne initially uses Scott to impress billionaire J.J. Jamison III (Bill Bixby), a playboy who owns Jamison Jammies and

Top: Have playground, will sing. But "Confidence," a thinly disguised remake of "High Hopes," is far from Presley's best children's number. Middle: Scott plots winning strategy with speedboat owner Sam Burton (Gary Merrill). Bottom: Boatbuilding a-go-go.

has won the last three Orange Bowl Regattas in his *Scarlet Lady* speedboat. And while Scott agrees to help her catch Jamison's eye, the more time he and Dianne spend together, the more Scott wishes she'd choose love over money. He therefore seizes the opportunity to impress her by competing against Jamison in the Orange Bowl International Power Boat Regatta.

Clambake was the first big-screen feature for director Arthur H. Nadel and screenwriter Arthur Browne Jr., two television veterans whose credits included episodes of *The Big Valley* and *The Rifleman* and other western series (which may explain why the name of Scott's speedboat is *Rawhide*). Nadel handles the dramatic and action scenes decently, but he stages *Clambake*'s musical numbers awkwardly, with little of the pizzazz that George Sidney brought to *Viva Las Vegas* (1964). So perhaps it's for the best that *Clambake* features fewer musical numbers than the average Presley film of the era. In fact, a pair of songs had to be added to the film's soundtrack album to fill it out: "Guitar Man" and "Big Boss Man." Aside from the title track, only a handful of *Clambake*'s songs linger in the memory, namely the ballad "A House That Has Everything," the go-go dance number "Hey, Hey, Hey," and "Who Needs Money," a duet featuring Presley and Hutchins, who had co-starred in *Spinout* (1966).

"Elvis throws the wildest beach party since they invented the bikini and the beat!"

— *Clambake* movie trailer and poster tagline

Dianne with billionaire J. J. Jamison III (Bill Bixby).

Dianne chooses love *and* money at the end of *Clambake*.

Nadel also neglects to evoke a sense of place in *Clambake*. Granted, much of the film was shot in Southern California (hence the mountains and oil wells in the background of many shots). And the footage he shot in Miami and the Florida Keys only used the actors' stand-ins. On the plus side, *Clambake* features exciting stock footage from the actual 1967 regatta race.

The film also benefits from having a strong supporting cast, with Gregory having a good ol' time as the filthy-rich elder Heyward, and Gary Merrill doing fine work as the owner of a speedboat company. Bixby also makes a vivid impression as Presley's arrogant rival for Fabares.

As for Presley, you'd never know how unhappy he was offscreen, because he's as sincere and charismatic as ever in *Clambake*.

SONGS IN CLAMBAKE

"Clambake"

"Who Needs Money"

"A House That Has Everything"

"Confidence"

"Hey, Hey, Hey"

"You Don't Know Me"

"The Girl I Never Loved"

STAY AWAY, JOE (1968)

MGM

DIRECTOR: PETER TEWKSBURY

SCREENPLAY: MICHAEL A. HOEY

BASED ON THE NOVEL BY DAN CUSHMAN

PRINCIPAL CAST: ELVIS PRESLEY (JOE LIGHTCLOUD), BURGESS MEREDITH (CHARLIE LIGHTCLOUD), JOAN BLONDELL (GLENDA CALLAHAN), KATY JURADO (ANNIE LIGHTCLOUD), THOMAS GOMEZ (GRANDPA), HENRY JONES (HY SLAGER), L.Q. JONES (BRONC HOVERTY) AND QUENTIN DEAN (MAMIE CALLAHAN)

Sweeping shots of Arizona's desert canyons, accompanied by a plaintive musical score, grace the opening credits of *Stay Away, Joe*. This artfully produced title sequence creates an expectation that Elvis Presley's 26th film will be a western drama in the vein of *Flaming Star* (1960), but *Stay Away, Joe* turns out to be broad, sophomoric comedy, awash in Native American stereotypes.

Presley stars as Joe Lightcloud, a Navajo rodeo rider whose parents, Charlie (Burgess Meredith) and Annie (Katy Jurado), live with Grandpa (Thomas Gomez) on an Arizona reservation. Determined to make a better life for his family, Joe convinces a congressman to give Charlie 20 heifers and a young bull to start a cattle-raising business. If Charlie succeeds, the government will create the same business opportunity for everyone on the reservation.

A brawling, fun-loving womanizer, Joe throws a big party to celebrate the launch of the family business.

Top: Arizona provides the stunning backdrop for *Stay Away, Joe*. Middle: Burgess Meredith as Charlie Lightcloud. Bottom: Joe Lightcloud (Presley) with his sister Mary (Susan Trustman).

Unfortunately, the drunken partygoers mistake the lone bull for a cow and barbecue it. Although another bull is obtained later, it only seems interested in snoozing, not breeding.

In between dalliances with Mamie (Quentin Dean), the sexy daughter of local tavern owner Glenda Callahan (Joan Blondell), Joe learns that his sister Mary (Susan Trustman) is engaged. When Mary decides to bring her future mother-in-law, Mrs. Hawkins (Anne Seymour), to meet the family, Annie starts selling off the cows to renovate the family's dilapidated house. With the entire government-provided herd sold off illegally, the Lightcloud family faces ruin and incarceration unless a way can be found out of the mess.

Directed by television sitcom veteran Peter Tewksbury, *Stay Away, Joe* marked the second time that Presley portrayed a Native American character on-screen; he had previously starred as the half-Kiowa hero of *Flaming Star*. But as Amy Cox writes in her essay on *Stay Away, Joe* for the website TCM.com, Presley took the role of Joe Lightcloud "to play a more sophisticated comedy role and hone his acting skills."

As Presley himself told an interviewer for *Cosmopolitan* during a break from filming, "You can learn an awful lot just by hanging out with real good professionals, and there isn't a day that goes by that I don't pick up something from the other actors." Indeed, *Stay Away, Joe* features some of Hollywood's most

Top: Joe warns Glenda Callahan (Joan Bondell) of an impending raid on her tavern. Middle: Joe puts the moves on Glenda's daughter Mamie (Quentin Dean). Bottom: Charlie, Annie (Katy Jurado) and Joe appraise their new bull.

revered character actors in pivotal roles, most notably Joan Blondell, Katy Jurado and Burgess Meredith. The epitome of a show business professional, Jurado broke some bones in her foot before shooting scenes, but rather than bow out of *Stay Away, Joe*, she gave her character a limp. That said, not everyone in the cast of *Stay Away, Joe* had such impressive acting credentials. Three members of Presley's "Memphis Mafia," Del "Sonny" West, Joe Esposito and Charlie Hodge, play small roles in the film.

Although Blondell, Jurado and Meredith do solid work in *Stay Away, Joe*, the film's most memorable performance is given by Thomas Gomez as Chief Lightcloud. With his deadpan delivery, Gomez effortlessly steals scenes — not that there's anything worth stealing in the finished product, which emphasizes crude, sexual innuendo–laced one-liners and sophomoric humor at the expense of genuine wit. In one scene, Presley serenades a bull with the song "Dominic" in the hopes that the bull will take a "romantic" interest in the heifers. According to author/Presley discographer Ernest Jorgensen, the star reportedly hated this song so much that he wanted it withheld from release. Presley's recording of "Dominic" would not be released until 1993, 16 years after his death.

Songs in Stay Away Joe

"Stay Away, Joe"

"Dominic"

"Lovely Mamie"

"All I Needed Was The Rain"

Top: Grandpa (Thomas Gomez, left) and Bronc (L.Q. Jones) hope they have resolved a problem facing their reservation. Bottom: Presley as the Navajo rodeo rider, Joe Lightcloud.

Two of Hollywood's finest character actors: Katy Jurado and Burgess Meredith in *Stay Away, Joe*.

To be fair, there are some amusing moments in *Stay Away, Joe*. What's offensive is the film's stereotypical depiction of Native Americans as lazy and dissolute. Whether *Stay Away, Joe*'s portrayal of Native Americans is racist, satirical or something in between is up to the viewer to decide. Most critics and audiences of the era agreed with *Variety's* reviewer, who wrote, "At best, film [*Stay Away, Joe*] is a dim artistic accomplishment; at worst, it caters to out-dated prejudice. Custer himself might be embarrassed — for the Indians."

Regardless of what the critics thought of, Presley seems to be having a good time on-screen as the brawling, skirt-chasing Joe. Such is the Presley charm that Joe comes across as likable, even at his most conniving. It's therefore all the more disappointing that *Stay Away, Joe* is such a misfire, both in terms of execution and in its depiction of Native Americans.

"The film's quaint and patronizing view of American Indians as brawling, balling, boozing children should rightly offend many."

— *Hollywood Reporter*

SPEEDWAY (1968)

MGM

DIRECTOR: NORMAN TAUROG

SCREENPLAY: PHILLIP SHUKEN

PRINCIPAL CAST: ELVIS PRESLEY (STEVE GRAYSON), NANCY SINATRA (SUSAN JACKS), BILL BIXBY (KENNY DONFORD), WILLIAM SCHALLERT (ABEL ESTERLAKE) AND CARL BALLANTINE (BIRDIE KEBNER)

The first thing viewers may notice in *Speedway* (1968) is how sleek and suave Elvis Presley appears in his 27th film, which has a sense of sheer, unadulterated fun, thanks to his winning chemistry with co-star Nancy Sinatra.

Once again cast as a race car driver, Presley portrays Steve Grayson, who uses most of his earnings to help other people, like Abel Esterlake (William Schallert), an impoverished widower struggling to raise five daughters. Whatever he doesn't give away, Steve spends to maintain his fairly lavish lifestyle, which revolves around chasing women with his manager and friend, Kenny Donford (Bill Bixby). That all changes once Steve meets beautiful IRS agent Susan Jacks (Nancy Sinatra) and learns that Kenny has gambled away much of his earnings. Unless Steve finds a way

Top: Abel Esterlake (William Schallert) accepts a gift from Steve Grayson (Presley). Middle: "You're looking me straight in the eye. That means you're lying." Steve wants the truth from his manager and friend, Kenny Donford (Bill Bixby). Bottom: A little problem with tax returns. Kenny and Steve hear the bad news from R.W. Hepworth (Gale Gordon).

to pay his back taxes, he'll lose everything — not to mention his shot with Susan.

As improbable as it may seem, *Speedway* was originally offered to Sonny and Cher. When it became a Presley star vehicle, the producers offered the female lead to British pop star Petulia Clark; Annette Funicello was also briefly considered for the role, which Nancy Sinatra ultimately took in what would be her final feature film. She also gets her own solo number in *Speedway*, the song "Your Groovy Self." It's the only song by another artist that ever appeared on an official Elvis Presley record.

Making his eighth Presley film in eight years, Norman Taurog does a commendable job on *Speedway*, which deftly blends production numbers with comic sequences. Then in his late sixties, Taurog was gradually losing his sight, yet summoned the wherewithal to direct *Speedway* and one more Presley film, *Live a Little, Love a Little* (1968), before retiring.

Speedway's effective racing sequences were filmed on location at racetracks in Concord, North Carolina, and Riverside, California. Ten cameras were employed to capture the exciting action in widescreen Panavision by cinematographer Joseph Ruttenberg. The four-time Academy Award–winning cinematographer whose credits included *The Philadelphia Story* (1940) and *Gigi* (1958) also shoots the film's costumes, sets and musical sequences in rich, eye-popping colors.

Top: "The check please." Susan Jacks (Nancy Sinatra), Steve and Kenny at a pivotal moment. Middle: Steve turns on the charm for Susan. Bottom: Sinatra and Presley make sweet music together in *Speedway*.

While Presley and Sinatra give *Speedway* its sizzle, a lively supporting cast provides the laughs. Fresh from playing Presley's nemesis in *Clambake* (1967), Bixby demonstrates a surprising facility for comedy as Kenny. And Gale Gordon, Lucille Ball's irascible foil on the sitcoms *The Lucy Show* and *Here's Lucy*, oozes officiousness as an IRS agent. Carl Ballantine as Grayson's chief mechanic and Burt Mustin as a janitor also contribute witty moments to *Speedway*, which features cameo appearances by real-life racers Buddy Baker, Dick Hutcherson, Tiny Lund, Richard Petty, G.C. Spencer and Cale Yarborough.

Released less than a month after the critically derided *Stay Away, Joe*, *Speedway* received surprisingly decent notices. *The New York Times'* Renata Adler enjoyed the film's "high lunatic moments" of comedy. Indeed, as film historian Stuart Galbraith IV notes on the website DVDtalk.com, *Speedway's* IRS-themed production number "He's Your Uncle, Not Your Dad" recalls "MGM's '50s musicals more than a late-'60s Elvis one."

Conversely, the *Chicago Sun-Times'* Roger Ebert complained that the Presley of *Speedway* "hold[s] no hint of the swivel hips my generation remembers from the Ed

"You're looking me straight in the eye — that means you're lying."

— Steve Grayson (Presley) to his friend and manager.

Steve in his stock car racing element. Presley also played a race car driver in *Spinout* (1966).

Richly colored costumes and splashy production numbers are part of the fun in *Speedway*.

Sullivan shows of 1956." Yet even as Ebert found the star "excessively proper" on-screen, he conceded that *Speedway* is "pleasant, kind, polite, sweet and noble."

For Presley, *Speedway* was the cinematic equivalent of a breath of fresh air; he comes across as energized and engaged by his role and seems to be enjoying himself immensely on-screen. It may not have revitalized Presley's Hollywood career, but *Speedway* is a cut-above most of the King's late 1960s-era films.

"Smooth, fast and in high gear."

— *Speedway* tagline

SONGS IN SPEEDWAY

"Speedway"

"Let Yourself Go"

"Your Time Hasn't Come Yet, Baby"

"He's Your Uncle, Not Your Dad"

"Your Groovy Self"

"There Ain't Nothing Like a Song"

LIVE A LITTLE, LOVE A LITTLE (1968)

MGM

DIRECTOR: NORMAN TAUROG

SCREENPLAY: MICHAEL A. HOEY AND DAN GREENBURG

BASED ON THE NOVEL "KISS MY FIRM BUT PLIANT LIPS" BY GREENBURG

PRINCIPAL CAST: ELVIS PRESLEY (GREG NOLAN), MICHELE CAREY (BERNICE/ BETTY/SUZIE/ALICE), RUDY VALLEE (LOUIS PENLOW), DON PORTER (MIKE LANSDOWN), DICK SARGENT (HARRY BABY), STERLING HOLLOWAY (MILKMAN) AND CELESTE YARNELL (ELLEN)

When Elvis Presley exploded on the scene as a performer and recording artist in the 1950s, he was viewed by some as a threat to moral values and the most dangerous man in America. He was certainly the sexiest man in the country for the next decade, although Hollywood took pains to tame and channel his ample sex appeal from animal lust into good-guy romance. But by 1968 the sexual revolution was in full swing, and Presley's unthreatening screen persona was a bit behind the times. *Live a Little, Love a Little*, the last of nine films Presley made with director Norman Taurog, marked a fascinating attempt to situate the star in an uninhibited world of scantily clad women and one-night stands. The story is set in anything-goes Southern California, but reflects the mores of attractive singles in big cities across the country, as promoted by then-reigning men's magazine *Playboy*.

Top: Shivering from his prolonged exposure in the ocean, Greg Nolan (Presley) has no choice but to accept the hospitality of his new "friend." Middle: Bernice (Michele Carey) gives Greg a pill to cure his fever. Bottom: Greg sings "Edge of Reality" in a dream sequence.

Indeed, the script was adapted from a novel by *Playboy* humorist Dan Greenburg, *Kiss My Firm But Pliant Lips*, that satirized publisher Hugh Hefner's image and lifestyle and had been serialized in the magazine's pages. The title, a parody of the era's trashy paperbacks like Jacqueline Susann's *Valley of the Dolls*, seemed too arch for a Presley film, so the producers went with the more generic *Live a Little, Love a Little*.

Another cultural and sexual touchstone of the day was referenced in the film's trailer. The line "It's a blowup . . . it's a blast!" alludes to the youth-culture notoriety of Michelangelo Antonioni's flamboyantly sexual and willfully ambiguous *Blowup* (1966), starring David Hemmings as a hedonistic fashion photographer in swinging London.

There's actually a little bit of Hemmings' fast-living *Blowup* protagonist in Presley's *Live a Little, Love a Little* character Greg Nolan. A newspaper photographer given to zipping his yellow dune buggy through the Pacific Ocean surf and sand, Greg is spotted by Bernice (Michele Carey), a sexy oddball one sun-baked afternoon. Within two minutes of meeting him, Bernice propositions Greg, lures him into her house and drugs him. By the time Greg awakens and flees a few days later, he's lost his job but found an ardent, if slightly kooky admirer in Bernice.

Top: Greg endures an embarrassing fitting session with the clothes-conscious head of the ad agency, Mr. Penlow (Rudy Vallee). Middle: Bernice's ex, Harry Baby (Dick Sargent), drops by to help his pals toast Greg's new house. Bottom: Greg directs a photo shoot for a girlie magazine.

In need of not one but two salaried gigs, Greg gets himself hired on as a photographer at a frisky men's magazine *and* an ad agency in the same building. Holding down two full-time jobs with the same hours requires a combination of resourcefulness and bravado that Presley conveys with disarming ease. Moreover, he infuses Greg with an unmistakably nonconformist spirit that sets him apart from both the buttoned-down agency executive Penslow (Rudy Vallee) and the Hefner-esque publisher, Mike Lansdown (Don Porter).

Greg is his own man from beginning to end, despite being outfitted in a stylish wardrobe of colorful, form-fitting pullovers and swank suits that correspond exactly to the well-groomed image that *Playboy* promoted in its pages in the 1960s.

With the lithe, lovely Carey (a child piano prodigy and top model turned actress) playing a genuine kook who changes her name as frequently as she switches outfits, *Live a Little, Love a Little* unfolds as a screwball comedy. Presley is compelled to play the straight man to Carey's unpredictable antics, but he takes control of the film during a pair of splashy production numbers: the enjoyably kitschy "Edge of Reality," staged as a dream sequence while Greg is drugged by Bernice; and "A Little Less Conversation," written by singer-songwriter Mac Davis, who would later contribute such gems as "In the Ghetto" and "Don't Cry, Daddy" to the Presley canon. In *Live a Little, Love a Little*, Presley sings "A Little

> "I adored Elvis. When I met him for the first time he immediately put me at ease. We had to film our kissing first and neither of us heard the director say, 'Cut!' For me, it was love at first kiss."
>
> — Co-star Celeste Yarnell

Greg informs Ellen (Celeste Yarnell) that he wants "a little less conversation, a little more action, please."

Greg and Bernice share a few moments of domestic bliss.

Less Conversation" to co-star Celeste Yarnell, who plays a lissome blonde he picks up at a swank party.

On a sober note, Yarnell's work on the film coincided with the assassination of Dr. Martin Luther King Jr. on April 4, 1968. During a lunch break, Yarnell joined Presley in his trailer to watch the telecast of Dr. King's funeral; the funeral of the slain civil rights leader reportedly moved Presley to tears.

Live a Little, Love a Little wrapped production on Elvis and Priscilla Presley's first wedding anniversary, May 1, 1968. A few days later, Presley began meeting with the executive producer of his upcoming NBC television special. In the course of planning and rehearsing for the show, Presley recorded a harder-edged version of "A Little Less Conversation," a confirmation of how much he liked the song. It wasn't used for the telecast, but nearly 35 years later, that take was remixed by the Dutch musician Junkie XL for a Nike advertising campaign, and "A Little Less Conversation" raced to the top of the charts in more than 20 countries.

Live a Little, Love a Little was the third Presley film released in 1968, after *Stay Away, Joe* and *Speedway*, none of which did more than middling business at the box office. His film career may have been at low ebb, but Presley wasn't ready to abandon Hollywood just yet.

SONGS IN LIVE A LITTLE, LOVE A LITTLE

"Almost in Love"

"A Little Less Conversation"

"Edge of Reality"

"Wonderful World"

CHARRO! (1969)

NATIONAL GENERAL PICTURES
DIRECTOR: CHARLES MARQUIS WARREN
SCREENPLAY: CHARLES MARQUIS WARREN
STORY: FREDERICK LOUIS FOX
PRINCIPAL CAST: ELVIS PRESLEY (JESS WADE), INA BALIN (TRACEY WINTERS),
VICTOR FRENCH (VINCE HACKETT), BARBARA WERLE (MRS. SARA RAMSEY),
SOLOMON STURGES (BILLY ROY HACKETT) AND JAMES ALMANZAR (SHERIFF
DAN RAMSEY)

Throughout his film career, Elvis Presley occasionally toyed with the idea of playing challenging roles in dramatic films. According to Hollywood lore, he was reportedly considered for a number of prestigious parts: John "Joker" Jackson in *The Defiant Ones* (1958); Brick in Tennessee Williams' *Cat on a Hot Tin Roof* (1958); Joe Buck in *Midnight Cowboy* (1969) and John Norman Howard, the over-the-hill rock star in the Barbra Streisand remake of *A Star Is Born* (1976). Regrettably, Presley squandered much of his cinematic potential by instead starring in a series of pleasant if forgettable musical romantic comedies. Before he bid Hollywood good-bye to focus solely on his musical career, however, Presley attempted to "stretch" as an actor one last time in the western *Charro!*.

Written and directed by Charles Marquis Warren, whose credits included the television westerns *Gunsmoke* and *Rawhide*, *Charro!* casts Presley as Jess

Top: Presley as former outlaw Jess Wade in *Charro!*
Middle: Vince Hackett (Victor French, right) gets the drop on Jess. Bottom: Jess is about to find out that a number of surprises lay in store for him.

Wade, a former outlaw in 1870s-era Mexico. Riding into a Mexican border town, Jess falls into a trap set by Vince Hackett (Victor French) and his crazed brother Billy Roy (Solomon Sturges). Ever since Jess left Hackett's outlaw gang to lead a law-abiding life, his former partners in crime have been plotting their revenge against him. They take him to a remote mountain hideaway where they've stashed the Victory Gun, a gleaming gold and silver cannon that fired the last shot against Emperor Maximilian I of Mexico; to make Jess pay for abandoning the gang, Hackett frames him for the theft of the Victory Gun.

Now a wanted man with a bounty on his head, Jess escapes to the small town of Rico Seco, the home of the only people he can trust: his former girlfriend Tracey (Ina Balin) and Sheriff Ramsey (James Almanzar). The Hackett gang soon arrives, setting the stage for a climactic showdown between Jess and Hackett.

A change of pace from the innocuous fluff he'd been making since the early 1960s, *Charro!* not only gave Presley his meatiest dramatic role since *Wild in the Country* (1961) — it also marked the first time he didn't sing on-screen. Indeed, the only song in the film plays over the opening credits. Another song, "Let's Forget About the Stars," was cut from the film.

Principal photography of *Charro!* began on location in Apache Junction, Arizona, at the Apacheland Movie

Top: Solomon Sturges (son of famed director Preston Sturges) plays the deranged Billy Roy Hackett. Middle: One of the rare moments in *Charro!* when Presley flashes a smile. Bottom: Tracey (Ina Balin) wonders if Jess has really changed his ways.

Ranch on July 22, 1968. Presley received $850,000 for his performance — more than half of the film's reported budget of $1.5 million — plus 50% of the film's profits. Filming concluded five weeks later on August 28, and *Charro!* was released the following year on March 13, 1969, following sneak previews in theaters across the Southwest.

Although the publicity machine went into overdrive for *Charro!*, with "*Charro! Girl*"contests in 25 cities, critics were generally dismissive of the film, which struck many as a poor man's version of a Sergio Leone "spaghetti western." Only Hugo Montenegro's score was praised, albeit begrudgingly, as an evocative if decidedly minor work by the composer of *The Good, the Bad and the Ugly* (1966).

As for Presley, he sadly seems uncomfortable in the role of the gunslinger; there are a handful of moments where he seizes command of the screen, yet there's a somewhat halting, muted quality to his portrayal of *Charro!*'s hero; he lacks the authentic gravitas that Clint Eastwood would have brought to the role. Presley also comes across as downright recessive opposite some of *Charro!*'s cast members, particularly Sturges (the son of the brilliant filmmaker Preston Sturges). Sturges chews the scenery in his wildly histrionic turn as the unhinged outlaw, Billy Roy Hackett; it's a shamelessly hammy performance that borders on parody.

In fairness, Presley doesn't have much to work with in *Charro!* The screenplay rarely rises above the level of a routine potboiler. Nor does he receive much help from director Warren, who hadn't made a feature film in

Top: Sara (Barbara Werle) takes care of her wounded husband, Sheriff Ramsey (James Almanzar). Bottom: Jess and Tracey get a second chance at romance.

Jess can't totally escape his criminal past.

years. His pedestrian, sometimes hesitant approach to the narrative drains the film of vital tension and momentum.

Despite the film's critical and commercial failure, *Charro!* nevertheless remains an interesting curio in Presley's film career — an intriguing but lackluster western that did not restore his dramatic credibility among critics and filmgoers.

THE TROUBLE WITH GIRLS (1969)

MGM

DIRECTOR: PETER TEWKSBURY

SCREENPLAY: ARNOLD AND LOIS PEYSER

BASED ON THE NOVEL "CHAUTAQUA" BY DAY KEENE AND DWIGHT BABCOCK

PRINCIPAL CAST: ELVIS PRESLEY (WALTER HALE), MARLYN MASON (CHARLENE), SHEREE NORTH (NITA BIX), EDWARD ANDREWS (JOHNNY), ANISSA JONES (CAROL), NICOLE JAFFE (BETTY), VINCENT PRICE (MR. MORALITY), JOYCE VAN PATTEN (MAUDE), PEPE BROWN (WILLY), DABNEY COLEMAN (HARRISON WILBY) AND ANTHONY TEAGUE (CLARENCE)

In an era when America was rife with political and social upheaval, Elvis Presley appeared in a film that focused on a much simpler time. *The Trouble with Girls* (1969) casts Presley as the manager of a traveling circuit Chautauqua, circa 1927. A circuit Chautauqua was a group of entertainers and speakers who traveled by rail from one small town to the next. Similar to a circus, a Chautauqua troop set up shop for a week to bring the arts, education, religion and recreation to people in rural areas. Although the Chautauqua Institution is still very active in its original, southwestern New York location, the circuit Chautauquas disappeared with the advances of communications and technology.

Stepping into a role originally intended for Dick Van Dyke, Presley portrays Walter Hale, the newly hired manager of a circuit Chautauqua. Arriving in Radford Center, Iowa, by rail, he is greeted by the town's entire population. Along with his business partner Johnny

Top: Johnny (Edward Andrews) and "the boss," Walter Hale (Presley). Bottom: Charlene (Marlyn Mason) accompanies Carol (Anissa Jones) and Willy (Pepe Brown) during their audition.

(Edward Andrews), Hale goes out into the crowd to drum up business. He gives tickets to two children, Carol (Anissa Jones, a.k.a Buffy of television's *Family Affair*) and Willy (Pepe Brown), and to Carol's grateful single mother, Nita (Sheree North).

Hale's slick charm and good looks seemingly impress everyone except Charlene (Marlyn Mason), the pretty director of the Chautauqua's children pageant. She's furious when Hale insists that she cast the mayor's talentless daughter in the pageant's lead role, rather than Carol; otherwise, Radford Center's mayor may withhold guarantee money. More amused than worried by her outburst, Hale tries to calm her, but his powers of persuasion initially fall on deaf ears; the pro-union Charlene informs him that he's violating the rules of her contract by overruling her casting decision.

Meanwhile, Nita annoys her married boss and lover, Harrison Wilby (Dabney Coleman), by leaving him to attend a Chautauqua lecture by Mr. Morality (Vincent Price). Wilby follows her and urges her to leave with him; when Nita refuses, he gets into a nearby card game that quickly goes sour.

The next day, a murder is discovered on the Chautauqua grounds. As rumors spread, the livelihood of the Chautauqua is threatened. Hale takes it upon himself to find the murderer, clear the name of the wrongfully accused *and* keep the Chautauqua profitable

Top: Hale performs a gospel song with one of his Chautauqua choirs. Middle: Nita Bix (Sheree North) and her domineering boss/lover, Harrison Wilby (Dabney Coleman) listen to a lecture. Bottom: Charlene argues the rules of the union.

and running. It's the proverbial tall order, but the charismatic Hale is more than up to the task; winning over Charlene, however, may take a little longer.

Although Presley has top billing in *The Trouble with Girls*, the film is very much an ensemble piece, as he is offscreen for considerable stretches of the film's running time. It's that rarity in Hollywood: a star vehicle that gives other cast members ample opportunity to create vivid characters. Among the familiar faces in the film's supporting cast, two actors stand out: Sheree North and Dabney Coleman. Briefly hailed as "the new Marilyn Monroe" in the 1950s, North had instead found steady work as a character actress in scores of film and television roles. Typically cast as a blowsy, down-on-her-luck aging glamour girl, she brings pathos to the character of Nita, who's trapped in an abusive relationship with Wilby, a prototypical snake oil salesman played with abrasive relish by Coleman. Then comparatively unknown, Coleman would achieve stardom 11 years later playing another smarmy bully, the nightmare boss in *Nine to Five* (1980).

Marlyn Mason, an actress who had enjoyed success on Broadway and in television, gives Charlene a bit more fire than the average love interest in a Presley film. Interviewed years later, she had only kind words for Presley: "Elvis got along with everybody and everybody loved Elvis." She also recalled that

> "The relations between negotiating parties can be better served by what is sometimes called 'getting into bed' with each other."
>
> — Walter Hale (Presley)

SONGS IN THE TROUBLE WITH GIRLS

"Almost"

"Clean Up Your Own Backyard"

Presley always addressed director Peter Tewksbury as "Mr. Tewksbury," even though director and star had previously worked together on *Stay Away, Joe* (1968).

Unlike most of his co-stars, Presley gives a rather low-key performance in *The Trouble with Girls;* he remains unflappable in the midst of chaos. As the *New York Times'* Roger Greenspun wrote in his mostly favorable review of the film, "Elvis Presley performs too, with a reasonably developed characterization … and he sings very well."

Many critics noted that the title of the film was a misnomer that had little to do with its content. Curiously, the film has a subtitle — *And How to Get It* — that is sometime used, i.e., on the DVD label, but does not appear in the film's title sequence. The working title of the film was *Chautauqua* (the title of the 1960 novel on which it's based), but concerns about the public's ability to pronounce this word of Seneca Indian origin convinced the powers-that-be to go with the more marketable, albeit misleading *The Trouble with Girls.*

However Presley's 30th film is known, *The Trouble with Girls* was the beginning of the end of the King's acting career. He would make just one more film, *Change of Habit* (1969), co-starring Mary Tyler Moore, before saying good-bye to Hollywood and returning to the concert stage.

Hale singing "Clean Up Your Own Back Yard" with a local band. Opposite page: "Negotiations" heat up between Charlene and Hale.

"The evocation of 1920's Americana is exceptionally even-handed, detailed, affectionate without sentimentality, funny without condescension."

— *New York Times* review

CHANGE OF HABIT (1969)

UNIVERSAL PICTURES

DIRECTOR: WILLIAM A. GRAHAM

SCREENPLAY: ERIC BERCOVICI, JOHN JOSEPH, JAMES LEE, RICHARD MORRIS AND S.S. SCHWEITZER

STORY: JOHN JOSEPH AND RICHARD MORRIS

PRINCIPAL CAST: ELVIS PRESLEY (DR. JOHN CARPENTER), MARY TYLER MOORE (MICHELLE), BARBARA MCNAIR (IRENE), JANE ELLIOT (BARBARA), LEORA DANA (MOTHER JOSEPH) AND ED ASNER (LIEUTENANT MORETTI)

In April 1969, Elvis Presley released the single "In the Ghetto," which rose to number three on the charts, his biggest hit since "Crying in the Chapel" four years earlier. So perhaps it is no coincidence that Presley would play an inner-city doctor in his final film, *Change of Habit*. Sporting longer, shaggier hair and mutton-chop sideburns, Dr. John Carpenter looks more rock star than physician and, indeed, when nurses Michelle (Mary Tyler Moore), Irene (Barbara McNair), and Barbara (Jane Elliot) report to their new boss, they find him singing to a group of enthralled teens. His reaction to them is equally confused, as he first assumes that they are uptown girls looking to his free clinic for one or more discreet abortions. He is more appalled to discover that they are his new helpers, sneering, "I ask for three hard-nosed nurses and they send three Park Avenue debutantes."

What John does not know is that the trio are really nuns in civilian disguise. "For once in our religious lives,

Top: Presley got rid of his signature pompadour to play inner-city doctor John Carpenter in *Change of Habit*.
Bottom: Dr. John Carpenter prescribes a dose of rock and roll to his teen patients.

we're not going to be different," Michelle insists. It is a stance that leads to all sorts of confusion. Their old biddy neighbors assume the young women are wanton party girls. A couple of Black Power advocates, Hawk (Ji-Tu Cumbuka) and Robbie (Bill Elliott), hassle Irene, suspicious of her friendship with white women. And jealous 17-year-old Desiree (Laura Figueroa) immediately sizes up Michelle as potential competition for the doc's affections. The teenager is not stupid, as John falls for Michelle.

Romance between the doctor and the sister is only one among myriad subplots in *Change of Habit*. Even music takes a backseat in this film. Presley slips into his old formula of randomly bursting into song only once, warbling the inane "Have a Happy," to Michelle and autistic child Amanda (Lorena Kirk) while riding a merry-go-round.

Instead of the fluffier-then-cotton-candy romantic musical comedy that had become the typical Elvis Presley vehicle, *Change of Habit* has more serious intentions. Into a scant 93-minute running time, it manages to squeeze in seemingly every urban ill and 1960s-era issue. Irene takes on the neighborhood loan shark (and apparent pimp) The Banker (Robert Emhardt). Barbara stages a sit-in at the grocery store over exorbitant pricing. Speech therapist Michelle acquires a stalker in Julio (Nefti Millet), the

Top: Out of their habits, Sisters Irene (Barbara McNair), Barbara (Jane Elliot), and Michelle (Mary Tyler Moore) make a bad first impression on Dr. Carpenter, who sizes them up as slumming uptown girls. Middle: Dr. Carpenter makes a house call with new nurses Michelle and Irene. Bottom: John feels the chill when he tries to make a move on Michelle. "I'm getting the feeling there's somebody else," he muses.

brooding Puerto Rican youth she treats for a stutter. The perils of racism, sexism, and poverty are infused into almost every frame. And while Vietnam is never mentioned, when John talks about an army buddy's battlefield death inspiring him to start the clinic, the inference is clear. While the nuns and John work to improve conditions in the neighborhood, none of them has any illusions about where they are. "Diplomacy starts at the end of a switchblade knife," is how John melodramatically puts it.

In fact, director William A. Graham was so intent on capturing some of the realism of the ghetto that he brought in real live rats to decorate his set. The idea backfired when the rodents got loose, forcing an evacuation of the soundstage. The director fared better in the verisimilitude department with his stars. There was no romance between Presley and Moore — according to Graham, it was Elliot who captured the King's amorous attention — but the singer adored his leading lady. "Elvis had a particular affinity for Mary and was a big fan of hers from *The Dick Van Dyke Show*," wrote his friend Sonny West. "He thought Mary was the total package: sexy, funny, talented, and extremely professional in her approach to her craft."

New York Times critic A.H. Weiler noted that *Change of Habit* was the 35-year-old Presley's 31st movie, a drama he deemed "merely exemplary of professional technique and dialogue rather than memorable characterization and emotion." Finding the story shallow yet overstuffed, the critic further adds, "Mr. Presley can't be faulted for remarking confusedly, 'I get a feeling there's a message here.' But it's only a slight and not terribly impressive one."

With Michelle's help, John reaches out to Amanda (Lorena Kirk), an autistic little girl.

SONGS IN CHANGE OF HABIT

"Change of Habit"
"Rubberneckin'"
"Let Us Pray"

"Man doesn't live by bread alone, especially the bread you can make workin' in a free clinic."

— Dr. John Carpenter (Presley) explaining why he was holding an impromptu concert in his examining room

By the time *Change of Habit* came out on November 10, 1969, Presley's musical comeback was complete. On November 1, "Suspicious Minds" hit number one on the *Billboard* pop chart, his first single to reach those lofty heights since "Good Luck Charm" in 1962. His Hollywood years were fading in the distance, while his Las Vegas years stretched out in front.

Who knows what might have happened had Presley continued in the movies?. He was reportedly offered the role of hustler Joe Buck in *Midnight Cowboy* (1969), which became the first and only X-rated film to win the Academy Award for Best Picture. With manager Colonel Tom Parker controlling Presley's decisions and more interested in soundtrack royalties than in letting his client develop as an actor, the serious movie career Presley desperately wanted never had a chance to develop.

Graham remembered Parker's contemptuous reaction when he found out the director was schooling Presley in improvisation and other acting techniques. "We make these movies for a certain price and they make a certain amount of money, no less and no more," Parker said. "Don't be goin' for no Oscar, sonny, 'cause we ain't got no tuxedos."

"My ambition has always been to become a motion picture actor — a good one, sir," Presley once told producer Hal Wallis. Instead, he found himself stuck in one frothy musical after another. *Change of Habit* may not come close to the ambitions of *Midnight Cowboy*, but at least Presley got to close out his movie career with something a little weightier than either *Harum Scarum* or *Clambake*.

"At the time, Elvis had the hairdo he was famous for. He had a kind of pompadour in front and his hair was full of grease. And because this was a movie about a doctor working in the ghetto, it just didn't seem to be quite the right hairstyle."

— Director William A. Graham explaining Presley's *Change of Habit* makeover

John's romantic dreams come crashing down with his first glimpse of Michelle in her nun's habit.

FILMOGRAPHY

Love Me Tender (1956)
Loving You (1957)
Jailhouse Rock (1957)
King Creole (1958)
G. I. Blues (1960)
Flaming Star (1960)
Wild in the Country (1961)
Blue Hawaii (1961)
Follow That Dream (1962)
Kid Galahad (1962)
Girls! Girls! Girls! (1962)
It Happened at the World's Fair (1963)
Fun in Acapulco (1963)
Kissin' Cousins (1964)
Viva Las Vegas (1964)
Roustabout (1964)
Girl Happy (1965)
Tickle Me (1965)
Harum Scarum (1965)
Frankie and Johnny (1966)
Paradise Hawaiian Style (1966)
Spinout (1966)
Easy Come, Easy Go (1967)
Double Trouble (1967)
Clambake (1967)
Stay Away, Joe (1968)
Speedway (1968)
Live a Little, Love a Little (1968)
Charro! (1969)
The Trouble with Girls (1969)
Change of Habit (1969)
Elvis: That's the Way It Is (1970)*
Elvis on Tour (1972)*

*Concert films